THE URGENCY OF IDENTITY

THE
URGENCY
OF
IDENTITY

Contemporary English-language Poetry from Wales

EDITED BY DAVID T. LLOYD

TRIQUARTERLY BOOKS
NORTHWESTERN UNIVERSITY PRESS
Evanston, Illinois

TriQuarterly Books
Northwestern University Press
Evanston, Illinois 60208-4210

Printed in the United States of America

ISBN 0-8101-5032-8 cloth
ISBN 0-8101-5007-7 paper

Library of Congress Cataloging-in-Publication Data

The urgency of identity : contemporary English-language poetry from
Wales / edited by David T. Lloyd.
    p.   cm.
"TriQuarterly books."
Includes bibliographical references and index.
ISBN 0-8101-5032-8 (alk. paper). — ISBN 0-8101-5007-7 (pbk. :
alk. paper)
    1. English poetry—Welsh authors. 2. English poetry—Welsh
authors—History and criticism—Theory, etc. 3. Poets, Welsh—20th
century—Interviews. 4. English poetry—20th century. 5. Wales—
Poetry. I. Lloyd, David T., 1954–
PR8964.U74 1994
821'.9140809429—dc20   94-9446
                                              CIP

For my mother

In memory of my father

▪ CONTENTS ▪

· ACKNOWLEDGMENTS ·

I wish to express my gratitude first to the writers represented in this anthology. Their friendliness and good humor—and devotion to their craft—made the editing of this anthology a pleasure. *Diolch yn fawr i bawb ohonoch.*

A travel-to-collections grant from the National Endowment for the Humanities and grants from the Research and Development Committee of Le Moyne College supported my work on this anthology. Le Moyne College also provided release time from teaching duties.

I drew parts of my introduction to this anthology from my article "Welsh Writing in English," which appeared in *World Literature Today* 66.3 (September 1992).

For advice during the various stages of this project, I would like to thank Cary Archard, John Barnie, John Bollard, Mick Felton, Patrick Keane, Margaret Lloyd, and Jonathan Schonsheck. For help with manuscript preparation, I am grateful to Lena Bertone, Vincent Boudreau, Sharon Knight, Judy Shoen, and Jennifer Stanley. It has been a pleasure to work with Reginald Gibbons, TriQuarterly Books editor for Northwestern University Press, and Susan Harris, my editor at Northwestern University Press: their enthusiasm and practical assistance helped steer this anthology from conception to completion. My mother, Mair Lloyd, deserves special mention for her work translating Welsh-language materials relating to this project. Finally, I owe a great debt of gratitude to Kim Waale for her encouragement, patience, and fine critical eye.

All poems appear by permission of the authors and their publishers. Most of the poems in this collection have been previously published as follows.

JOHN DAVIES: sonnets 1, 2, 6, 8, 9, 11 of "The Visitor's Book," "In Port Talbot," and "Regrouping" from "The White Buffalo" were previously published in *The Visitor's Book* (Poetry Wales Press, 1985); "Farmland" was published in *Flight Patterns* (Seren Books, 1991).

GILLIAN CLARKE: "Plums," "Fires on Llŷn," "Seal," "Windmill," and "Neighbours" were published in *Letting in the Rumour* (Carcanet Press, 1991); "Sheila na Gig at Kilpeck," "Llŷr," and "Blodeuwedd" in *Selected Poems* (Carcanet, 1985).

NIGEL JENKINS: "First Calving," "Snowdrops," "Parc," "Castell Carreg Cennen," and "The Patient" were published in *Acts of Union* (Gomer Press, 1990).

JEAN EARLE: "The Tea Party" was published in *A Trial of Strength* (Carcanet Press, 1980); "Jugged Hare," "Faithless Dreams," and "Afterwards" in *Selected Poems* (Seren Books, 1990); "Visiting Light" in *Visiting Light* (Seren Books, 1988); "Old Tips" and "The Garden Girls" in *The Intent Look* (Gomer Press, 1984).

OLIVER REYNOLDS: "Dysgu" and "Daearyddiaeth" were published in *Skevington's Daughter* (Faber & Faber, 1985); "One would Think the Deep to be Hoary," "Dispossessed," and "L. M. C. 1890" in *The Player Queen's Wife* (Faber & Faber, 1987); "Clarinet" and "Full Circle" in *The Oslo Tram* (Faber & Faber, 1991).

CHRIS BENDON: "Constructions" was published in *Constructions* (Gomer Press, 1991); "Swansea" was published in *Software* (Spectrum, 1984).

CHRISTINE EVANS: "Small Rain," "Whale Dream," "Power," and "Second Language" were published in *Cometary Phases* (Seren Books, 1989).

TONY CONRAN: "Wild Form" and "Elegy for the Welsh Dead, in the Falkland Islands, 1982" were published in *Blodeuwedd* (Poetry Wales Press, 1988); "Giants," "Counting Song," "Caernarfon Across Brown Fields," and "Gwales" in *Castles: Variations on an Original Theme* (Gomer Press, 1993).

RUTH BIDGOOD: "Kindred," "Gale," "Banquet," and "Image" were published in *Kindred* (Poetry Wales Press, 1986); "Speech" in *Lighting Candles* (Poetry Wales Press, 1982); and "Llanfihangel" in *Selected Poems* (Seren Books, 1991).

DUNCAN BUSH: "The Hook," "Ramsey Island," "Living," and "Summer 1984" were published in *Salt* (Poetry Wales Press, 1985).

JOHN BARNIE: "Optional," "Parallel Lines," "I Can't Keep Them Both," "Out of the Fight," "Phantoms," "The Town Where I Was Born," and "At Craig-y-Pistyll" were published in *The Confirmation* (Gomer Press, 1992).

MIKE JENKINS: "The Common Land" and "Chartist Meeting" were published in *The Common Land* (Poetry Wales Press, 1981); "Invisible Times" in *Invisible Times* (Poetry Wales Press, 1986); "Gurnos Boy" and "Returning to the Nant" in *A Dissident Voice* (Seren Books, 1990).

ROBERT MINHINNICK: "The Looters," "Development Area," "'What's the Point of Being Timid When the House Is Falling Down?'," "The Mansion," "The Stones Themselves," and "Looking for Arthur" were published in *The Looters* (Seren Books, 1989); "The Drinking Art" in *Native Ground* (Christopher Davies Publishers, 1979).

SHEENAGH PUGH: "The Frozen Field," "The haggard and the falconer," and "Frankincense" were published in *Selected Poems* (Seren Books, 1990); "Railway Signals" in *Beware Falling Tortoises* (Poetry Wales Press, 1987).

TONY CURTIS: "Pembrokeshire Seams" and "Jack Watts" were published in *Letting Go* (Poetry Wales Press, 1983); "The Death of Richard Beattie-Seaman in the Belgian Grand Prix, 1939" in *Selected Poems 1970–1985* (Poetry Wales Press, 1986); "Midnights" in *The Last Candles* (Seren Books, 1989).

CATHERINE FISHER: "Immrama," "St Tewdric's Well," and "Snakebite" were published in *Immrama* (Seren Books, 1988).

PETER FINCH: "The Speaker," "Block," and "Rubbish" were published in *Selected Poems* (Seren Books, 1987).

HILARY LLEWELLYN-WILLIAMS: "Birch" and "The Cruelest Month" were published in *The Tree Calendar* (Poetry Wales Press, 1987); "To the Islands," "Brynberllan," "Nola," and "The Inner Artificer" in *Book of Shadows* (Seren Books, 1990).

R. S. THOMAS: "R.I.P" and "A Marriage" were published in *Mass for Hard Times* (Bloodaxe Books, 1992); *Counterpoint* (1990) was published by Bloodaxe Books.

David T. Lloyd
November 1993

· INTRODUCTION ·

Over the last seventy years English-language poets of Wales, drawing from the colonizer's language but writing out of a Welsh cultural milieu and environment, have created a literature comparable in its originality and vitality with any other arising from a colonial or postcolonial condition. This impressive literary awakening is all the more dramatic because of its being scarcely noticed—much less celebrated or studied—outside the borders of Wales. Contemporary English-language poetry from Wales is a legacy and a continuation of a movement seeded in the 1920s and reaching a "first flowering" during the 1930s and 1940s with the publication of such poets as Alun Lewis, Lynette Roberts, Idris Davies, and Dylan Thomas; and a "second flowering" during the 1950s and 1960s with the poetry of R. S. Thomas, Raymond Garlick, Roland Mathias, John Tripp, and Harri Webb. But while most readers of poetry in North America are aware, for example, of Dylan Thomas's reputation and poetry, few know much of the range and richness of contemporary poetry from Wales—or of the essential fact that Wales is home to two literatures and two languages. In *The Urgency of Identity*, readers will find some of the best recent English-language poetry from Wales.

To provide a forum for the most current poetry, I have restricted my selection to works published since 1980 (though a few unpublished poems are also included). Except for R. S. Thomas and Tony Conran, I did not include poets who established reputations during the 1950s and 1960s, so that those first coming into prominence during the 1970s and especially the 1980s could be more fully represented. This decision necessitates the absence of influential "second flowering" poets still active in the English-language literary culture of Wales but allows for the inclusion of younger poets who are instilling that culture with a new vitality.

Four interviews are interspersed among the poems to help establish a literary and cultural context for readers not familiar with poetry from Wales or with publishing conditions specific to Wales. In the first interview poet Gillian Clarke discusses her experience of living, writing, and editing a literary magazine in a "land of two languages." While Clarke's interview addresses

Welsh writing in English from the perspective of a poet born and raised in Wales, Jeremy Hooker's interview relates the impressions of an outsider—an English poet and critic sympathetic to, and for many years involved in, the developing English-language literary scene in Wales. In the third interview, John Barnie—a poet, essayist, and editor of the influential magazine *Planet, the Welsh Internationalist*—challenges the characterization of contemporary Welsh writing in English as a body of work separate from English literature. The fourth interview, with Meic Stephens, Director of the Literature Committee of the Welsh Arts Council from 1967 to 1991 and editor of numerous poetry anthologies, provides an overview of the growth of English-language literature in Wales during the past three decades.

As with poets from other cultures in a colonial or postcolonial condition, most contemporary English-language poets of Wales experience—consciously or unconsciously—an ambivalent relationship to the English language: it is their language but not, historically, the language of their culture. For many of these writers, literary production in English rather than in Welsh compromises their sense of national identity—or constitutes, to phrase the problem in blunt terms, a kind of treason. I have titled this anthology *The Urgency of Identity* to highlight the attention given by poets in Wales to this political and literary issue.

■　■　■

In Wales, the issue of identity is inseparable from the issue of language. From its origins in a poetic tradition reaching back to the sixth century, Welsh literature was composed primarily in the Welsh language, though in different periods writers of Welsh origin or provenance also wrote in Latin, French, and, with increasing frequency, English. But by the early decades of the twentieth century enough Welsh men and women were speaking, reading, and writing primarily in English, especially in the south of Wales, to give birth to a new literature. To understand the development and current status of Welsh writing in English, one must first know something of Welsh culture and Welsh-language literature—for whatever makes English-language writing from Wales distinct from English literature proper must relate to the degree of its "Welshness," however that might be defined. Also, modern Welsh-language and English-language writers of Wales have been—and still are—very conscious of the actual and the potential tensions and conflicts resulting from the presence of two language communities within a single nation. That consciousness has exerted a powerful influence on the development of Welsh writing in English.

It is not widely known outside Britain that distinctive and vibrant Welsh-language culture and literature have survived despite English control of governmental, religious, and educational institutions since Edward I's defeat of Llewelyn ap Gruffydd, the last native prince of Wales, in 1282. Wales was formally annexed to England through the Acts of Union of 1536 and 1543, which enacted a number of language restrictions, mandating, for example, that only English could be used in law courts and only Welshmen who spoke English could hold public office.

Reasons for the decrease in the number of Welsh speakers over the last two hundred years have been extensively analyzed and documented, and include economic, political, and educational factors.[1] The comparative resilience of the Welsh language through the eighteenth and nineteenth centuries, when related minority languages—Manx, Scots Gaelic, and Irish Gaelic—were in precipitous decline, has also been described in a number of studies.[2] The sharp decline in numbers of Welsh speakers in the twentieth century began with the massive influx of English-speaking immigrants seeking work in the coal and iron industries of south Wales at the end of the nineteenth and through the early decades of the twentieth centuries. The census of 1901 documented the first time this number fell below fifty percent; the number is lower in each subsequent census, leveling off only during the last decade. The struggle to preserve the Welsh language—and so preserve Welsh literature and culture—continues, though with fewer of the direct action campaigns against oppressive language laws of the 1960s and 1970s, when language protestors were regularly put on trial for civil disobedience and, occasionally, violence.

Despite centuries of pressure towards anglicization in Wales, novels, critical and scholarly works, and collections of poetry continue to be published in the Welsh language, reviewed in Welsh-language newspapers and literary journals, and discussed in Welsh on Radio Cymru. A Welsh-language television channel, *Sianel Pedwar Cymru* (channel 4, Wales), has broadcast news, cultural programs, and even soap operas and game shows from the capital city of Cardiff since 1982, when proponents of Welsh-language TV won a decade-long battle with Prime Minister Thatcher's government over the issue.[3]

A variety of political organizations have developed during this century to oppose the anglicizing pressures on Welsh-language culture. These include Plaid Cymru (Party of Wales), a nationalist party founded in 1925, which is represented in the British parliament but seeks Welsh independence, and organizations working to preserve and extend the Welsh language, such as Cymdeithas yr Iaith Gymraeg (Society for the Welsh Language), which employs civil disobedience in its language campaigns.[4] There is also a more extremist dimension to Welsh nationalism: Meibion Glyndŵr, a shadowy militant group, claims responsibility for the fire-bombing over the last twelve years of hundreds of English-owned holiday homes in the heartland of Welsh Wales (events referred to in John Davies' poem "Fires").[5] Today, less than one-fifth of the 2.8 million people living in Wales speak Welsh. Although the Welsh language has gained new vitality in recent years, it is still a minority language under siege, whose survival through the next century is far from certain.[6]

Those who see Welsh literature in English as distinct from provincial English literature argue that the sensibilities of its writers have been fundamentally shaped by the Welsh culture, landscape, and language. Poet, critic, and translator Tony Conran, for example, argues that interaction "between the two language-groups of Wales" occurs "on all cultural levels."[7] While it is difficult to ascertain the extent, or even the existence, of complex and subtle cultural interactions, one powerful force—the Welsh language itself—has certainly shaped and will continue to shape English-language literature in Wales and attitudes toward that literature. A few Welsh writers in English have Welsh as their mother tongue; some have acquired the language as adults; others speak little or no Welsh. No matter what their relation to the Welsh language and its literature, all Welsh writers are affected by the tensions between the two literatures and cultures. Speaking or writing Welsh communicates cultural—even political—allegiance, which partly accounts for the significant number of contemporary English-language writers who have learned, or are learning, the language.

The term "Anglo-Welsh" itself reflects the complexities of literary and cultural identity in Wales. Coined by H. Idris Bell in 1922 to refer to Welsh writing in English, it was in common use by the 1930s[8] and actively promoted during the 1950s and 1960s to distinguish that literature from, and give deference to, Welsh-language literature. Though still in use, the term is rejected by some writers and critics for its implications of divided national allegiance and an acceptance of colonial linkage to England.[9] This political dimension has led many writers to prefer the term "Welsh writer in English" to "Anglo-Welsh writer."

Modern Welsh literature in English was, in fact, born out of a political environment. The coal-producing valleys of south Wales, centers of labor unrest and left-wing agitation during the 1920s and 1930s, provided the intellectual and artistic ferment out of which many of the "first flowering" English-language writers developed. Idris Davies and Glyn Jones, writing poetry, and Jack Jones and Gwyn Thomas, writing short stories and novels, are acclaimed early representatives of valleys writers working in English.

The "second flowering" during the 1960s was spearheaded by a group of committed nationalists, including Tony Conran, Meic Stephens, and Harri Webb. Stephens founded the Triskel Press in 1963 and *Poetry Wales* magazine in 1965 to "provide a conduit for a consciousness of Wales through the English language."[10] It was the 1960s and 1970s that saw English-language literature firmly established in Wales, with its own publishing vehicles and Welsh Arts Council financial support and with a clear nationalistic bias. Today, three literary magazines (*The New Welsh Review*, *Planet*, and *Poetry Wales*) and two presses (Gomer Press and Seren Books) publish the great majority of English-language poetry and fiction appearing in Wales.

For complex reasons, Welsh writing in English has not gained recognition, much less acceptance, easily, neither within Wales nor abroad. It is written out of a Welsh milieu, physically and culturally distant from the centers of English-language literary activity in London and New York. At the same time, this literature is often seen as peripheral—even antithetical—to the culture and literature of Welsh-speaking Wales, despite the nationalist political sympathies of many English-language authors. It has been a tenet of modern Welsh nationalism—in particular of Plaid Cymru and Cymdeithas yr Iaith Gymraeg—that the continuity of the Welsh language is an integral element of political independence and viable nationhood. In this context, the existence of an English-language literature in Wales can be viewed positively, as a vehicle of nationalist expression for the English-speaking Welsh, or negatively, as one more assault upon Welsh-language culture.

Clearly, the presence of two languages and two literatures raises contentious questions in present-day Wales. Can one be Welsh without speaking Welsh? Can there be a Welsh literature not written in the Welsh language? Will English-language literature in Wales—"Anglo-Welsh literature"—necessarily lose its distinctive qualities over time to become a regionalist branch of English literature? The term "Welsh poetry" itself projects different meanings depending on context: defined linguistically, "Welsh poetry" refers to poetry written in the Welsh language; defined geographically, it can refer to poetry in English or Welsh written within the borders of Wales.

■ ■ ■

Not surprisingly, these politically charged language/identity issues surface as compelling subject matter for the poets in this anthology. Gillian Clarke, who has learned Welsh, finds that living in a land with two languages enlarges a writer's available resources. Poets such as Clarke and Tony Conran integrate elements of the Welsh culture, literary tradition, and mythology in their poems, as in Clarke's "Blodeuwedd" and Conran's "Elegy for the Welsh Dead in the Falkland Islands, 1982." In her poem "Llŷr," Clarke connects a childhood experience of watching *King Lear* at Stratford in England with her adult knowledge of Llŷr, a figure from Welsh mythology and literature and a distant prototype of Shakespeare's Lear. Shakespeare gave voice to "rhymes about sorrow," remembered by the poem's speaker thirty years later in the transforming context of a Welsh environment and a consciousness informed by the history, literature, and mythology of Wales.

John Davies, who does not speak Welsh, must be listed among the poets urgently concerned with identity issues, in particular with the dislocation and alienation attendant upon loss of language. In his poem "Farmland," Welsh words are "familiar foreign words," yet in poem 11 of "The Visitor's Book" Davies uses "we" and "us" to refer to the Welsh people and their shared history: "What can castles say to us except that, / once, we were too weak to squeeze them flat?" Davies' situation vis-à-vis his family life and the Welsh language is emblematic of the fragmentation of Welsh culture: while Davies' wife and daughter are Welsh speakers (as was his father, now deceased), he and his mother do not speak Welsh, a circumstance referred to in sonnet 9 of "The Visitor's Book." A similar concern with identity and loss of language motivated Cardiff poet Oliver Reynolds to write of the complex emotional and psychological experience of learning Welsh (see his poems "Dysgu" and "Daearyddiaeth"). Not all poets of Wales, however, address identity/language issues directly. Some, such as Tony Curtis, consciously avoid them. While much of Curtis's poetry celebrates the people and places of south Wales, in particular the Gower Peninsula and Pembrokeshire, more recent poems reach insistently beyond Wales, exploring historical events in India or Europe, as in "The Death of Richard Beattie-Seaman in the Belgian Grand Prix, 1939."

As a group, the writers in this anthology reflect concern with national identity by rooting their poems in specifically Welsh times and places. Everywhere in Wales one confronts emblems and remnants of the deep and the recent past: the megalithic tombs, standing stones and stone circles, Iron Age hill forts, Roman roads, ruined abbeys, Norman towers, Edwardian castles, waste heaps of coal and slate, and the vast derelict steelworks near Port Talbot, once the largest and most productive in the world. It is thus not surprising that Welsh poets as a whole are intensely interested in mythology and in history, ancient and modern. In poems by Tony Conran, English-built castles—one of the great tourist attractions of Wales—are potent symbols of a defining historical fact: military occupation and cultural/economic subjugation of the Welsh by the English. In poems by John Barnie, Nigel Jenkins, and Christine Evans, bombers and fighter planes streak over ancient hill forts and castles. This incongruous juxtaposition of the modern and the ancient reminds one not only of the profound danger and instability inherent in the contemporary period but also of the continuing status of Wales as a subject nation: these war planes are American or British, not Welsh. In Barnie's poem "Phantoms," warplanes are objects of deadly beauty, gazelles whose leap into the air is a deeply ironic "act of grace." The Phantom jet provides an apt metaphor for Welsh history, embodying warfare, invasion, and wrenching cultural dislocation, as well as unexpected continuity into the modern era.

While an historical perspective encompassing centuries informs a number of poems in this anthology, many other poems address very contemporary social, economic, and political conditions. Mike Jenkins, for example, sets many of his poems in contemporary Merthyr Tudful in south Wales, where he lives and teaches. Much of his work presents a social and political context that will be unfamiliar to those who think of Wales in terms of its natural beauty or its Celtic associations. Once the heart of Britain's coal mining and iron industries and a hotbed of labor-related political agitation, especially during the nineteenth and early twentieth centuries, Merthyr Tudful now suffers some of the worst unemployment in the United Kingdom. Robert Minhinnick's poetry also undertakes explorations of the south Wales valleys, one of the earliest environments to be ravaged by industrial pollution, slag heaps, and relentless urban development.

The poet who represents the highest achievement of contemporary English-language poetry from Wales is undoubtedly R. S. Thomas, whose life and writings embody the politically charged issues of cultural and linguistic identity in Wales. Of his twenty-four poetry collections published to date, I have selected from two of the most recent, *Counterpoint* (1990) and *Mass for Hard Times* (1992). An outspoken nationalist who has learned Welsh and lives in an area with one of the highest concentrations of Welsh-speakers (the Llŷn peninsula), Thomas yet feels unable to write poetry in any language but his first—English. He describes his painful struggle with the dilemma of writing in English while remaining politically committed to the Welsh language and culture in his essay, "The Creative Writer's Suicide."[11] While Thomas's poems over the last five decades have been shaped by the political and cultural context particular to Wales, they are free of parochialism, addressing large themes of moral responsibility and difficult choice. Finely crafted, authoritative, grounded in place and time yet wide ranging in theme, they are, quite simply, important poems for the contemporary world.

This introduction can provide only a brief survey of some literary and cultural issues raised by the poetry in *The Urgency of Identity: Contemporary English-language Poetry from Wales*. Readers will discover their own pleasures and interests as they experience individual poems. But they will also learn something of the hold that Wales, as a country, a culture, and a loved place, exerts on her poets. "*Beth yw'r ots gennyf i am Gymru?*" ("What does Wales matter to me?") asks T. H. Parry-Williams in his poem "Hon" (which can be translated as "This"). "*Nid yw hon ar fap / yn ddim byd ond cilcyn o ddaear mewn cilfach gefn*" ("On a map / this land is only a piece of earth in a back corner").[12] Yet the pull of this "piece of earth" on Welsh poets of both languages is fierce: "*Ac mi glywaf grafangau Cymru'n dirdynnu fy mron,*"

Parry-Williams concludes, "*Duw a'm gwaredo, ni allaf ddianc rhag hon*" ("I feel the claws of Wales tearing my breast. / God save me, I cannot escape from this").[13]

THE URGENCY OF IDENTITY

· JOHN DAVIES ·

FROM "THE VISITOR'S BOOK"

1

Just where along the line did this voice start
chirping *cheerio* and *chap*, my language
hopping the frontier? Things fall apart,

the sentry cannot hold. Distant, he will keep
barking 'Where d'you think you are, boy? On stage?
Back of the gwt!' My cover, see, isn't deep.

My ear/year/here sound suspiciously the same.
Should I say 'I'll do it *now*', don't bank on it.
And, upstarts, some new words seem assumed names:

brouhaha sounds like the Tory Hunt tearing fox
-gloves. *Rugger* too. I can't say *Dammit*
or ride phrases trotting on strong fetlocks.

These days, language slouching through me lame
from the States is—well, a whole new ballgame.

2

Cymmer Afan: wet pensioned streets fagged-out
claim only drifting is possible here.
At journey's end, no surge but smoke, no sound
from the deep except some lorry's threshing.

I was towed dreaming on this stretch years back,
a boxed childhood bobbing between high walls.
Then steel's fist pulled the plug on coal
so I was flushed down to Port Talbot.

No, on the whole I don't think I'd go back—
though I do for the usual half-reasons
and took my daughter once. Like me, perhaps
she'd pick up the sonar blips. Nettle-stung,
she proved only the seer's point that one's
Lost Valley is just another's vale of tears.

6

Dusk. My road shadows the ghost railway track.
Tunnelling homewards, streets smoke twists of string.
I think of Idris Davies who, mists back,
lit up these valleys with poems signalling
the flame must not go out. They kindled each
other, words and people. But old hat, agreed,
and just as well that now he's out of reach.
Who cares which moths on musty clothing feed?

It's nice though that at least a special case
has been made for Viscount Tonypandy's
robes at Cardiff Castle, a special place.
The loyal stockings, too, which warmed his knees,
the wig even, that became his head so well—
how they'll enjoy controlled conditions still.

8

To swerve from village chapel to a town's
high-stepping church is, in midfield caught,
to feel life-forces collide, one woodbrown
and squat, all Welsh (my father must have thought
I'd catch faith like the measles), that tall other
dazzling in a blonde-haired surge of incense
with etiquette's deft sidesteps my mother
introduced me to. Pity, I made no sense
of either. And announcements—usually
in Ostrich—from the pulpit's grandstand failed

to clear up the game's essential mystery.
Even now I am not sure what I've missed.
From bare boards, sudden, to brass altar rail:
it's partly the shock has kept me atheist.

9

The t.v. set, stirring itself, confides
in my father in Welsh. Bored, I can see
outside the steelworks signal in the sky
to streets speaking pure industry.

His first language I did not inherit,
a stream my father casually diverted
to Cymmer clean past us all. Brisk shifts
of my mother's tongue worked in my head.

My wife and daughter speak it, strumming
on green places, a running water-beat
beyond me. But though I've picked up some
of the words, they do not sound like mine.
It is like hearing what might have been.
Pointless to mourn that far-off rippling shine.

11

The *Year of the Castles*, and we are hosts
to flag-makers, tourist boards, sly 'sham ghosts'.
What can castles say to us except that,
once, we were too weak to squeeze them flat?

Its ramparts strolled by slate-capped streets,
an unvisited hill fort became my seat
where over-anxious mist hauled down the hills.
It couldn't stop what is advancing still.
History, we learned, was mostly Royal chaps
and chapesses joined in blurred mishaps.

Well, still their castles stand up anyhow.
And wave. And since my walls are breached, by now
I've had to scratch inside inviolate space
at last for pieces of the starting place.

In Port Talbot

By now it's like returning to a foreign town, especially
at night when the steelworks' familiar fever
flushes again faint red on walls and ceilings.
Its reverberations, too, this time I cannot hear
as silence. When cars stop smashing rain to spray
or after a train has dragged its chains across stone floors
what remains is this, work's dying murmur.

Lying flat, the whole town breathes through stacks;
gouts of asthmatic coughing churn the sky.
All night in burnt air, an enormous radio
aglow with coiled circuits, aerials straining high,
blasts out selections from Smoke at ranked streets
with floatings of thick chords that echo for miles.
They drown, almost, the groundswell hum nearby.

Homes of the well-off on Pentyla have the best view
of the steelworks. The main road follows it obediently.
Running coastwards greased by rain, streets skidded
to this edge, finding metal had replaced the sea
with slabs that rear white-ridged with steam then stop.
All night, rolling in over the beached town
are breakers never seen, a thrumming like memory.

Look out on winter's thin streets. See how steel
lights up the whole town still. Although it shivers now
in November dreaming of steel's breaking point, its people—
kept from clean air but not each other—could tell how
common purpose, gathering, runs strongest
on hardest ground. As here where the land turned
overnight to metal, where smoke blooms in the window.

And when at last shared work's vibrations cease,
sharing itself will fade (as in the mining villages nearby)
with Keir Hardie's dream, with Bethanias long since ghosts,
down history's shaft. Difference and indifference will untie
taut bonds of work that cramp yet forged here a community;
then old South Wales will have to start a New. Meanwhile
reverberations still, slow leavings, long goodbye.

Regrouping

As a boy Joe Washington had cigarettes
stubbed on his tongue. Now an old man
at the pow-wow downtown, he speaks
in the common currency. But sings in Salish.
Each winter the Nootcka floods his shack.
Winter again, language of willows pours
downstream on his niece dead, loss
greening loss till sharing sings him home
and the drumming starts, the dancing.

I go outside to smoke.
'We gave tobacco, the whites whisky.
Lung for a liver—fair exchange'.
The thrum of hunched drummers is wiped out
by trucks like warehouses sliding east.

Between dances a cop keeps raiding
the microphone. No drinking, check
your children. Holds up a knife he's found.
The watchers, passive or impassive, watch
and I think of a plane crash, survivors
of flung seats stunned who keep regrouping.

This singing in another tongue old anthems
in a shared redoubt, I've no part in.
But am not apart. I have been here before
elsewhere, just visiting from a century
aging faster than time that has said no
to so much now there's just money,

John Davies   9

as though inside might be someone or
something I'd half-known and lost.

Farmland

Inland from the English-speaking sea,
where I lose my bearings and my wife translates,
market towns gather villages.
Henllan, Trefnant, Llanrhaeadr had come
past trees brushing mist from the fields
to Denbigh's plantation of telegraph poles.

Steps stood up, and high arched doors
checking again familiar faces
narrowly took me in. On her aunt's
coffin, flowers had drained the light
but not those packed pews: murmurs, ripples
were refilling farmland's hollows.

The minister's shock of eyebrows
hedging raw cheeks, he'd have hauled a ram.
Speech shook me off. It was tenors
gliding on familiar foreign words in search
of thermals drew me towards the woman
gone, to Joe who doesn't speak Welsh

or often, relying on closed ranks.
Once connection tunes its instruments,
feeling's airborne over fact
and, soaring, forgets it still bears

language asserting difference, how else
leap snags of common ground?

At the coast were fingers of cloud
all bruises and gold rings. Caravans
made one thin road an anywhere.
What we travel from also moves from us,
and gulls guarding clutches of pebbles
turned into people briefly then flew off.

FROM "READING THE COUNTRY"

1. Penmon (for Ieuan Wyn)

We left the quarry town still tunnelling.
Roofless, men roofed cities with what they'd found.
What were they looking for? Where the Straits swing
open, it seemed far off, that ripped headland
whose priory also broke new ground.
I'll have your poems translated, I said.

In uncrowded air, a buzzard wavered,
casually tightrope walking. Then flew on
through your language and mine blurred
wordless in the skimming towards Penmon
as if rock's undertow had been washed green
of the faults words still try fathoming, thrown
by the eye over so much space between
us, so much spanning it, above, below.

John Davies   11

2. Cwmorthin

It has emptied, that bowl of a valley
hung cracked in Blaenau's draughty rafters, true.
It isn't empty now. Some rework slate.
And the new roads that make all secrets free
send weekend ski jackets glittering through
along paths half a century out of date.

A while back, the mute chapel's disbelief
flared white into graffiti: *Twll din*
pob Sais and *FWA*. They're fading though.
Trails thicken. It stares like the old chief—
scarfaced, somewhere innocent of wheels
till foraging newcomers cast shadows—
who asked how many, how many more are . . . ?
and the answer was, 'Like the stars'.

14. Fires

Soon 'insignificant homes were burning,
the suburbs of tiny ants,' as Hooson
the poet saw fire ransack dry fern.
It might have been, 'in heaven's calm eyes', loosed
upon Rome while a madman's fiddle croaked.
Or Bosnia? crackle airwaves. We are
decades on, between ants and clouds, smoke
tainting cool air. Heaven's a mind too far.

Still, distance measures not just miles
nor even the efficiency of eyes.
Here now, if you want, over a wide sweep,
you can see only a blue haze enchant
Glyndŵr country between the Conwy's sleep
and Llŷn's arm pointing towards Ireland.

29. The old language

is yours if your word for home means 'here'.
Whatever it nudges from retirement,
sharp-eyed, beckons lost worlds words nearer.
It can make more connections than were meant.

Streams clear the throats of derelict caves
to deliver rivers that have outgrown
ruin fluently in slate villages,
in towns that are mills still dressing the flow.
Here isn't home. And does not sound (riches
pour past!) much like my country, though it is.

Echoes outlast sound. Listen, nudged awake,
they too murmur. Says earth's vocabulary
of names on scribbled surfaces: it takes
more than the one tongue to speak a country.

▪ GILLIAN CLARKE ▪

Plums

When their time comes they fall
without wind, without rain.
They seep through the trees' muslin
in a slow fermentation.

Daily the low sun warms them
in a late love that is sweeter
than summer. In bed at night
we hear heartbeat of fruitfall.

The secretive slugs crawl home
to the burst honeys, are found
in the morning mouth on mouth,
inseparable.

We spread patchwork counterpanes

for a clean catch. Baskets fill,
never before such harvest,
such a hunters' moon burning

the hawthorns, drunk on syrups
that are richer by night
when spiders pitch
tents in the wet grass.

This morning the red sun
is opening like a rose
on our white wall, prints there
the fishbone shadow of a fern.

The early blackbirds fly
guilty from a dawn haul
of fallen fruit. We too
breakfast on sweetnesses.

Soon plum trees will be bone,
grown delicate with frost's
formalities. Their black
angles will tear the snow.

Fires on Llŷn

At sunset we climb Uwchmynydd
to a land's end
where R. S. Thomas walks, finding
the footprint of God
warm in the shoe of the hare.

Words shape-shift to wind,
a flight of oystercatchers,
whinchat on a bush,
two cormorants fast-dipping wings
in a brilliant sea.

Over the holy sound
Enlli is dark in a ruff
of foam. Any pebble or shell
might be the knuckle-bone
or vertebra of a saint.

Three English boys throw stones.
Choughs sound alarm.
Sea-birds rise and twenty thousand saints
finger the shingle
to the sea's intonation.

Facing west, we've talked for hours
of our history,
thinking of Ireland
and the hurt cities,
gunshot on lonely farms,

praised unsectarian saints,
Enlli open
to the broken rosary
of their coracles,
praying in Latin and Welsh.

Done with cliff-talking
we turn inland, thinking
of home silently filling
with shadows, the hearth
quiet for the struck match,

our bed spread with clean sheets.
Our eyes are tired
with sun-gazing. Suddenly
we shout—the farms burn.
Through binoculars we see

distant windows curtained with flame.
The fires are real
that minute while we gasp,
begin to run, then realise
windows catch, not fire but

the setting sun. We are struck still
without a word
in any language. See the hares run,
windows darken,
hear the sea's mumbled novenas.

Windmill

On the stillest day
not enough breath to rock the hedge
it smashes the low sun to smithereens.

Quicker than branch to find a thread of air
that'll tow a gale off the Atlantic
by way of Lundy, Irish Sea.

At night it knocks stars from their perches
and casts a rhythmic beating of the moon
into my room in bright blades.

It kneels into the wind-race
and slaps black air to foam.
Helping to lower and lift it again

I feel it thrash in dark water
drumming with winds from the Americas
to run through my fingers' circle

holding the earth's breath.

Neighbours

That spring was late. We watched the sky
and studied charts for shouldering isobars.
Birds were late to pair. Crows drank from the lamb's eye.

Over Finland small birds fell: song-thrushes
steering north, smudged signatures on light,
migrating warblers, nightingales.

Wing-beats failed over fjords, each lung a sip of gall.
Children were warned of their dangerous beauty.
Milk was spilt in Poland. Each quarrel

the blowback from some old story,
a mouthful of bitter air from the Ukraine
brought by the wind out of its box of sorrows.

This spring a lamb sips caesium on a Welsh hill.
A child, lifting her face to drink the rain,
takes into her blood the poisoned arrow.

Now we are all neighbourly, each little town
in Europe twinned to Chernobyl, each heart
with the burnt fireman, the child on the Moscow train.

In the democracy of the virus and the toxin
we wait. We watch for bird migrations,
one bird returning with green in its voice,

glasnost
golau glas,
a first break of blue.

Sheila na Gig at Kilpeck

Pain's a cup of honey in the pelvis.
She burns in the long, hot afternoon, stone
among the monstrous nursery faces
circling Kilpeck church. Those things we notice
as we labour distantly revolve
outside her perpetual calendar.
Men in the fields. Loads following the lanes,
strands of yellow hair caught in the hedges.

The afternoon turns round us.
The beat of the heart a great tongue in its bell,
a swell between bone cliffs; restlessness
that sets me walking; that second sight
of shadows crossing cornfields. We share
premonitions, are governed by moons
and novenas, sisters cooling our wrists
in the stump of a Celtic water stoop.

Not lust but long labouring
absorbs her, mother of the ripening
barley that swells and frets at its walls.
Somewhere far away the Severn presses,
alert at flood-tide. And everywhere rhythms
are turning their little gold cogs, caught
in her waterfalling energy.

Llŷr

Ten years old, at my first Stratford play:
The river and the king with their Welsh names
Bore in the darkness of a summer night
Through interval and act and interval.
Swans moved double through glassy water
Gleaming with imponderable meanings.
Was it Gielgud on that occasion?
Or ample Laughton, crazily white-gowned,
Pillowed in wheatsheaves on a wooden cart,
Who taught the significance of little words?
All. Nothing. Fond. Ingratitude. Words

To keep me scared, awake at night. That old
Man's vanity and a daughter's "Nothing",
Ran like a nursery rhythm in my head.

Thirty years later on the cliffs of Llŷn
I watch how Edgar's crows and choughs still measure
How high cliffs are, how thrown stones fall
Into history, how deeply the bruise
Spreads in the sea where the wave has broken.
The turf is stitched with tormentil and thrift,
Blue squill and bird bones, tiny shells, heartsease.
Yellowhammers sing like sparks in the gorse.
The landscape's marked with figures of old men:
The bearded sea; thin-boned, wind-bent trees;
Shepherd and labourer and night-fisherman.
Here and there among the crumbling farms
Are lit kitchen windows on distant hills,
And guilty daughters longing to be gone.

Night falls on Llŷn, on forefathers,
Old Celtic kings and the more recent dead,
Those we are still guilty about, flowers
Fade in jam jars on their graves; renewed
Refusals are heavy on our minds.
My head is full of sound, remembered speech,
Syllables, ideas just out of reach;
The close, looped sound of curlew and the far
Subsidiary roar, cadences shaped
By the long coast of the peninsula,
The continuous pentameter of the sea.
When I was ten a fool and a king sang

Rhymes about sorrow, and there I heard
That nothing is until it has a word.

Seal

When the milk-arrow stabs she comes
water-fluent down the long green miles.
Her milk leaks into the sea, blue
blossoming in an opal.

The pup lies patient in his cot of stone.
They meet with cries, caress as people do.
She lies down for his suckling, lifts him
with a flipper from the sea's reach
when the tide fills his throat with salt.

This is the fourteenth day. In two days
no bitch-head will break the brilliance
listening for baby-cries.
Down in the thunder of that other country
the bulls are calling and her uterus is empty.

Alone and hungering in his fallen shawl
he'll nuzzle the Atlantic and be gone.
If that day's still his moult will lie
a gleaming ring on sand
like the noose she slips on the sea.

Blodeuwedd

Hours too soon a barn owl
broke from woodshadow.
Her white face rose
out of darkness
in a buttercup field.

Colourless and soundless, feathers
cream as meadowsweet
and oakflowers, condemned
to the night, to lie alone
with her sin.

Deprived too of afternoons
in the comfortable sisterhood
of women moving in kitchens
among cups, cloths and running
water while they talk,

as we three talk tonight
in Hendre, the journey over.
We pare and measure and stir,
heap washed apples in a bowl, recall
the day's work, our own fidelities.

Her night lament
beyond conversation,
the owl follows
her shadow like a cross
over the fields,

Blodeuwedd's ballad
where the long reach
of the peninsula
is black in a sea
aghast with gazing.

· INTERVIEW WITH GILLIAN CLARKE ·

DL: Your recent writing is much more concerned with political rather than strictly personal subjects. I'm thinking of poems such as "Neighbours" or "Fires on Llŷn," from *Letting in the Rumour*. Can you speak some about that shift in focus?

GC: My recent poems show a wider engagement with the world. My first book, *The Sundial*, was very domestic because I was at home, and domestic life was pressing to be expressed, life with the children. Once I moved to live in Cardiganshire in 1984, I no longer had a child at home. My youngest son was eighteen, and so off he went, and that was it. Nineteen eighty-four was the year of my move away from the family. My children are still important to me, but now they are responsible for themselves. At that time, I began to allow myself to become more interested in things like green issues, science, the New Nature, the winds and the weathers, coming from somewhere and going to somewhere. Our prevailing weather is Atlantic weather. So there's a sense of being one with the world. How can we help but feel more interconnected? Now, I don't feel British at all. I'm Welsh and European. I may live out on the Western fringe of Europe, but I feel extremely involved in it.

DL: In your recent poetry, you seem to have been moving more deeply into Wales, yet simultaneously extending yourself from Wales.

GC: Yes I am. I've put down even deeper roots here, which is where my family came from. So you meet me here in the Welsh heartland instead of the house in Cardiff, where I spent most of my life and where I lived when I wrote my first two books. *Letting in the Rumour* was written here, in Cardiganshire.

DL: Most of your early poetry has been in the form of the short lyric, but recently you've been working with the long poem, as with "Cofiant" and "Letter from a Far Country." Why does the longer poem appeal to you?

GC: Only when reading or writing a long poem or a poem sequence do you get the sense of diving deep down and at last surfacing weeks later as if you've been underwater. It's an extraordinary experience, whereas the little poems just come as they might. For those big ones you go off by yourself and shut the door, and don't talk to people. I suppose it's a bit like writing a fast novel. How you can continue to write a novel over a period of a year I cannot imagine. I can imagine the total involvement of working on a short novel because that's exactly how I work with a long piece. I wrote "Letter from a Far Country" in about five nights. I wrote "Cofiant" in a week, though my thoughts on both had been with me for years. I must say, I enjoy an intense period of writing very much, but when you're not doing it, you can't imagine how you could do it. I can't imagine doing it right now.

DL: "Letter from a Far Country" was commissioned by *Planet* and "Cofiant" by the BBC. Do you find commissions appealing?

GC: I like to be forced to work. I had a very interesting experience recently at the Hay-on-Wye Festival. About six writers were invited, given a subject upon arrival, spent the weekend writing, and reported on the results. The subject—Border: Fatherhood, Motherhood—was right up my sleeve because Hay-on-Wye lies on the border between Wales and England. "Fatherland" threw some of the writers, because it reminded them of the last war with Germany. But for me, fatherland was where my father came from and motherland was where my mother came from. It was simple. At another level, it was physical: the fatherland in me and the motherland in me. The father in me and the mother in me. Internal and external landscapes. I enjoyed writing under pressure and wrote something I was pleased with. I think it's the beginning of the next long poem. Commissions force me to stop staring out the window, making coffee, cleaning the windows, saying, "I think I'll make jam today."

DL: Some of the writers I have interviewed commented that the best English-language writers of Wales gain their poetic strength through being in touch with their Welshness. Do you find that so?

GC: There is no choice. I am Welsh. Wales is a small country with a culture under pressure, and being Welsh is one of the tensions that provokes me to write.

DL: There are poets such as R. S. Thomas or Harri Webb who don't want any part of an Anglo-Welsh literature. Are you experiencing any of those negative feelings?

GC: That is their way of describing the tension. My feelings about it are more positive. I live in a land with two languages. Twice as lucky. It's a delicate situation which we've landed in. Here's an example. I chair the Taliesin Board for Tŷ Newydd.[1] Obviously we serve two languages. For me Welsh is a second language. In the company of academics or Welsh writers, I feel more at ease speaking English. Some members of the Board speak no Welsh at all, and I have to ask each speaker to translate after speaking, or I have to do it myself. At the end of the day, I'm exhausted with the effort of thinking in two languages, one which I speak well and the other which I speak considerably less well. This is what it is to be Welsh: it is sometimes bilingually confusing. It's head splitting, but it's worth it. It's an edge. There's no moment of life in Wales that hasn't got that edge, unless you decide you're not Welsh. Some people think all that's too difficult: "It's not what I want, I want to be me in the modern world." I would think that some younger writers have taken this position: "I want to be a mid-Atlantic writer." It's painful to all of us. There are people who live here, in this area of Wales, who might as well be living in the London suburbs: they're not in Wales at all. That doesn't include all those who don't speak Welsh, but it includes all those who don't accept the fact that Wales is different.

DL: Does the idea of an Anglo-Welsh literary tradition going back many centuries make sense to you?

GC: For me it doesn't, though I find it interesting. Ieuan ap Swrdwal's "Anglo-Welshness" is less important than Dafydd ap Gwilym's genius.[2] I'm interested in the best poets. And many of the early ones happen to be Welsh-language writers. I had to learn Welsh because I could not be excluded from the language of Dafydd ap Gwilym. The term "Anglo-Welsh" implies mixed ancestry, which I have not got. Or it implies that there is an Anglo ascendancy, as in Anglo-Irish, which not true of Wales, historically.

DL: Which writers in English have you been interested in?

GC: Everything R. S. Thomas writes is interesting. He's more prolific than any other writer in Britain. Has any British poet of substance written so many books? Ted Hughes also. But I also love the work of Seamus Heaney and Michael Longley. Lately my constant companions have been the work of Derek Walcott and of the fine Irish woman poet Eavan Boland.

DL: I haven't been aware of much interaction between Irish poets and Welsh poets, in terms of Welsh writers being published in Irish magazines, or Irish writers in the Welsh magazines.

GC: I'm published in some Irish magazines. And I've read in Belfast and been to Ireland a few times for readings. How many others have, I'm not sure, though there is certainly a great interest in the poets who write in Welsh. Menna Elfyn is popular in Ireland.

DL: You're one of the first of a significant number of women now publishing poetry in English in Wales.

GC: There are many good women writers. Jean Earle is wonderful. Have you heard her read? She's in her eighties, and a beautiful woman in a quiet, silvery way. She's very up to date and modern in her thought. Christine Evans is another writer whose work I admire.

DL: What do you think has opened up publishing in Wales for women?

GC: The quality of their writing. When I edited the Poetry Book Society anthology in 1987, there were fifty poets in it, and twenty-five of them were women. In 1986, the editor had six women in the anthology. In 1988, there were about ten women. In 1991 Anne Stevenson restores the balance again. I didn't do it on purpose when I was editor; I just chose the best of the poets. It's not to do with subject matter but with a way of seeing. My taste led me to those poets. If the editors are men, their sensibilities naturally turn towards what they favor, what they enjoy and respond to. A poet like Seamus Heaney has a tremendously feminine sensibility, and because Seamus Heaney is such an extremely good poet, he admitted possibilities that weren't there before, which women are now exploring. To put it another way, more women began to be published, which enabled us to see a poet like Seamus Heaney. I wonder whether he would have been as well received by an earlier generation, when feminine values were less noticed and admired.

DL: How did you first come to have poems published?

GC: I threw my first poems in the bin because I was unaware they were poems. I suppose it was because I hadn't read anything in print that was like what I was writing. I think we all need models, and I was both Welsh and a woman. The world wasn't very interested in either. Have you noticed how late in their careers women get published? Both Ruth Bidgood and Jean Earle, whose work I like, were published late in their lives. I read *Poetry Wales*, and I saw things there that spoke to half of me, the Welsh part. It would never have occurred to me to send work to London. My former husband posted some poems off to *Poetry Wales* because I had said, "I could write as well as this." Meic Stephens, the editor at that time, wrote back accepting them.

DL: When you assumed editorship of *The Anglo-Welsh Review*, after sharing editorship with Roland Mathias, in what ways did the character of the magazine change?

GC: I put poetry first, and I cared more about the appearance of the magazine. I wasn't as academic—I'm not as scholarly as Roland. He's an historian and an astute scholar. I'm a creator, not a scholar. I put poetry first because it's what I like best. If I were editing a magazine now, what I'd really like to have is just fiction and poetry.

DL: What kinds of editorial criteria did you use?

GC: I chose what I liked. I sometimes put in poems that I didn't like but recognized as good poems. I might read a collection, thinking, what can I learn from this? What do I want? Why don't I like this? What's wrong with me? Quite a few books at the moment seem to me to be totally lacking in music. Not unmusical in the right, American way; not unmusical in the William Carlos Williams way. Not unmusical in that competent language that knows where it's going. It's something else, which I don't enjoy. In fact, on the whole I do not enjoy contemporary English poetry. The young ones, the new ones coming along, I haven't liked any of them. Maybe it's my fault. I'm still trying.

DL: Did you consciously promote Welsh writing as an editor, or would you publish just the best of what came in?

GC: It would be just the best, but more Welsh people sent work in than English, and very often, English people sent their worst poems. They sent poems about holidays in Wales, buying a holiday cottage, or some other subject which is likely to remain unpublished. If a promising poet was Welsh, I would take more notice of the work—I suppose there was that kind of prejudice, but I didn't count the poems. I just thought, "This is interesting. From a Welsh poet, too. This one could get better. Wait a minute, we've got something here."

DL: Are you working on any new projects at present?

GC: Well, the border piece I spoke of in connection with the Hay-on-Wye festival, and I'm working on the script of a BBC film, partly autobiographical, partly statement.[3] We'll be filming at the place where my father's family came from. And that, by chance, is the place I've been writing my poems about lately.

DL: You've been doing a lot of work in writing and education. Do you experience any conflict between writing and teaching?

GC: No. It's a creative whole. Poetry's for everyone. One of my ambitions in life is to destroy the prejudice that says poetry is just for the few. That doesn't mean that what everybody writes is publishable. But the engagement—trying to write poetry, reading poetry, becoming literate, becoming more aware of poetry—is for everyone. We don't say that rock music isn't music, we say it's rock music. If we go on making these distinctions—this is a poem; this isn't a poem—we will continue to bar the population from taking an interest in it, whereas everybody, or nearly everybody, listens to music. Almost everybody has a cassette player. Or a walkman. Who hasn't got a walkman? Poetry should also be for everyone.

• NIGEL JENKINS •

First Calving

Up through the rain I'd driven her, taut
hocks out-sharing a streak of the caul,
and that single hoof, pale as lard,
poked out beneath her tail.

In shelter,
across the yard from me now,
her rump's whiteness fretted the dark.
I watched there the obscure passage
of men's hands and, exiled in crass
daylight, waited—

                    till a shout
sent me running big with purpose
to the stable for a halter.

They flipped to me the rope's end, its
webbing they noosed around the hoof:
we leaned there, two of us, lending weight
to each contraction; the other fumbled
for the drowning muzzle, the absent leg,
  said he'd heard that over Betws way
    some farmer'd done this with a tractor—
      pulled the calf to bits and killed the cow.

Again she pushed, and to first air
we brought the nostrils free; next the head
and blockaging shoulders, then out
he flopped, lay there like some bones pudding
steaming with life.

            Later,
she cleansed. I grubbed a hole in the earth
and carried the afterbirth out
on a shovel: to be weighted with a stone,
they said, to keep it from the scavengers.

Parc

Here he set his English elms
& his cattle and his deer,

& hereby over all
with stones hewn by his cousin the Norman
      did he raise in artful wildness
        the ruin of a tower,

from close under heaven enjoying command
of all lands sound, sweet & fertile
        'twixt the bounteous sea

& those sour, safely distant, Welsh-speaking hills.

The new man, cruising the sward in his Rolls,
        farms it through the bank.
Brambles root mid-field, the fencing sags
as he waits on a deal or permission to build.
You can hear through the crows the throats
he sits on, see in flung gateways the mouths
        his farming fails to feed.

I watched through one summer
his elm trees die. No May will plump
this copse with shade, an ending is here,
        it is time to re-plant.
But this man will not, nor any of his kind.

Something beyond him is taking its course.

The Patient

To continue on this earth
you have only but often
to place in your mouth
a little piece of the world
—an apple, a fish—
& let it move through you

depositing good
till that moment at dawn
when it steams back into light
with a stench so exquisite
it cannot be shared.

I'd follow now as always
this rule of freedom
—it is not Calcutta,
there are luxuries of food—
but the world is refusing
to travel through me:
the bile stinks,
week by week I am
getting lighter:
if it weren't for the pain
I'd float clean away.

Castell Carreg Cennen

Castell Carreg Cennen: helmet wrought
from the crag's limestone
to glower on Deheubarth: the brain
flown, twisting now in hideous freedom
to western sun & the strip at Brawdy.

To stand under shadow:
of stone's relentless sophistication, the word
Nagasaki: & no sudden white bird
on the darkening below

nor the sun's choosing of the faces of farms
can draw the soul from its coldness.

Today's invaders, a busload from Swansea,
their grey heads and hats like hydrangeas
lost in thistle, found among fern
as they straggle to the top.
. . . *& every Wednesday, the mystery voice . . .*
broody talk—of radio routines,
of cakes & curtains &
letters home from daughters & sons—
counterpoints description
of improved methods of waging war,
counterpoints rattle of the single cup
in the houseful of rooms.

. . . *the mystery voice, at 8.55 & again*
at twenty-five minutes past nine . . .

Fresh eggs for sale in the farm below; they
linger, buying, & as we head for the bus
one of them hands me a clutch
of three—though what she says
there's no hearing, language
robbed from her mouth by a screaming jet.

Three fresh eggs:
warm in my palm long after the fighter
has rumbled into silence
through the arming skies.

Snowdrops

I know what I am doing here,

come every year
in the iron first month

to seek them out.

I choose my time,
a day to freeze
the waters of the eye,
and I move through it

—primal caver delving in sign—

to link with light
of the living blood.

■　■　■

Last year too soon,

not a white word
in all the wood's deadness.

Home then speechless

to wait.

■　■　■

Sky grey and lowering
curtains the wood:

no money, no food: hush
of alone here, cold
of hunger,

last place of warmth
a hole in the head
that's known, I remember, as mouth.

■　■　■

A man in a coat
hunting flowers.

Sudden scatty cackle—
the waving of a branch:
a magpie, I trust, has left the tree.

Here, now
the blue gift amazing
of kingfisher flight

would not be believed.
I ask only

snowdrops,
a warmer world.

■ ■ ■

A warmer world?

■ ■ ■

And here they nod
in the cold and quiet.

In Bolivia the soldiers
broke glass on the ground.
They made the naked children
lie flat on the glass,
they made the mothers walk
on the children's backs.

Here snowdrops nod
in the quiet and cold.

If the bomb fell on Swansea,
fifty miles away in Cardiff
eyeballs would melt . . .

Can
    a flower?
Can
    the poem?

■ ■ ■

Brother dead in Paviland:

the first I pick
I pick in celebration
of the species that stayed
when all others fled
the coming of the cold,

species now trembling
through a darker season
of its own manufacture.

■   ■   ■

Feet gone dead, hand around the stems
some borrowed thing, a clamp
of frozen meat

but

tlws yr eira

blodyn yr eira

cloch maban

eirlys

lili wen fach

—a song in my fist.

■　■　■

The owl is with her
the day's length,
and she is sick
of the moon:

her winters are long.

I hand her snowdrops:
she grasps the primrose.

■　■　■

Inside from the cold
they boast no bouquet,

just green breath
of the earth's first things.

I find them a glass,
and on the worktable
scattered with papers
I place them

It is enough.

■　■　■

Thin sun creeps
upon the afternoon

and the water warms,
bubbles sprout
on the earthpale stems.

They'll die early, yes,
and drop no seed:

the year may live.

■ JEAN EARLE ■

Jugged Hare

She mourned the long-ears
Hung in the pantry, his shot fur
Softly dishevelled. She smoothed that,
Before gutting—yet she would rather
Sicken herself, than cheat my father
Of his jugged hare.

A tender lady, freakish as the creature—
But resolute. She peeled it to its tail.
Oh, fortitude! Her rings sparked in and out
Of newspaper wipes. Blood in a bowl,
Sacrificial gravy. A rarely afforded
Bottle of port.

She sustained marriage
On high events, as a child plays house.

Dramas, conciliations—
Today, the hare. She sent me out
To bury the skin,
Tossed the heart to the cat.

She was in full spate.

Fragrance of wine and herbs
Blessed our kitchen; like the hare's dessert
Of wild thyme; or like his thighs
As though braised by God. She smiled
And dished up on willow,
Having a nice touch in framing
One-off scenarios.

After the feast, my father was a lover
Deeply enhanced.
I heard them go to bed,
Kissing—still inside her picture.
Later, I heard her sob
And guessed it was the hare
Troubled her. My father slept,
Stunned with tribute. She lay now
Outside her frame, in the hare's dark

Hating her marital skills
And her lady-hands, that could flense a hare
Because she wooed a man.
In years to come,
I understood.

Afterwards

The surviving half of the earth
Shuddered: centred the sun:
Went on turning.

With that year's decline
The migrant birds
Followed their stars
To alternate summer
And the steadied trades
Carried such butterflies and moths
As make these odysseys—mindless
Whether they journeyed as birds or insects

For some were effortless travellers,
Catching a lift, duveted against windwarps
By stronger flyers. Within each skull—
Insect or bird—
Delicate, fierce magnets
Locked on the goal, moving in cloud
Or vee formations,
To the summer land.

Likewise, through immemorial
Byeways of seas, fishes and eels
Urgently pressed towards the birth-rivers.

And there was nothing. . . .

Nesting materials
Nor caterpillars, nor the inherited dance
Of ephemera, nor the expected
Certain alighting places.

The home waters ran no taste
Of arrival. Manifestations of death
Clogged in the bays. By natural law,
No U-turn possible. . . . . .

They hovered while—
Sensing some predatory cull
More ruthless than usual—
Till the overstretched wings
Weakened and fell. The insect pheromones
Received no messages. On the bad tides
New phosphorescence
Dulled—and stank.

That was the season when there were—for once—
No human predators.

Faithless Dreams

Sometimes, in dreams, we meet our souls'
Perfectly matched shells,
Linked at the dreamer's hasp: shone through
With heat glowed from a lucent dark
Between curves. Even while we coil about
Sleeping companions, the shells close,
Melting the quick.

Sense of the ridiculous,

In serious dreams, deserts us.

I and this civil servant (bowler, umbrella)

Phosphorescent nudes on a station

Clocked with farewells. We were not sad,

Knowing we'd meet again. Other disguises—

But the dream, basic.

Once, drifting to a wedding,

Early; the dream confused with miners

Going to work. Catching them up,

He walked with me, instead. Nineteenth-century

Pit gear this time. Cap over eye.

The sun rose remorseless

Over village and mountain. We lay in the shade

All day. I never got to the wedding

Nor he to shift. Married (he said)

And I, Promised. . . . Yet we were guileless

As Dante and Beatrice, young and untouched.

I, in her red dress . . .

We need not value our homes and day-loves

Less for it; nor feel guilt on waking . . .

For surely, those with whom we share

Beds and sleep, also have their dreams?

The Tea Party

I asked my dead to tea.
Accumulated news pointed my tongue
Like a pin through silks, like a crammed bee-bag,
Heavy to unload.

They sat in the garden,
Smiling the stone-burnt roll-call of their names.
I set a table between roses,
Laid with their favourite things.

Oh, my sweet dead—the cakes, the cakes!
All news discharged to the faint, receptive sheen
Of your listening eyes. Then, for the first time
I knew that you were dead at last, and I—

Healed?

It came upon me with the emptied teapot
And the westering sun. I had no plans for you
Beyond the afternoon.

Old Tips

Over the years, a tip would take on time's finish,
A greening over—
Seen from far off, a patina
As on bronze memorials. It was a feature
Of place and weather, one of the marks of home

To my springloaded people.

Autumn in the allotments; sunlit on high,
The town shadowed. All the pits asleep.
Sometimes, cows off a neglected farm
Would stray across a very old tip—
Lie around on the strange, wispy grass,
Comforting their udders.
Old tips breathed out a warm, greenish smoke
After rain,
Suggesting thin, volcanic pastures.

Some tips were famed as wicked, secreting runnels
Of dark, treacle death; swallowing houses
Helpless at their feet.
But most were friendly—
We children ran out of school
Visiting the one that rose
Close to our playground.
We scrambled towards the top—
To shriek the dandelion flaring in the grit
And that abandoned crane,
Pointing to the annual sea.

The Garden Girls

During the eighteenth and nineteenth centuries, women of Wales—especially in Cardigan-shire—used to migrate to London to work in the parks. They were known as "Merched y Gerddi"—"The Garden Girls."

Movements on a land—single
Then run together like ants, wildflowers.

The great Bog. The sky.

Spring migrants, following paths
Of the Old Peoples.
Banks crusted with cattle hairs, the Roman roads
Under rain and sun.

Wave, to the hill farms, hanging down poor fields. . . .

In wake of the drovers; on foot, by pillion and cart,
Skirts excited beyond prudence, eyes shining
Above mud and dust with the excitement of it. . . .
Some had been before and knew the ways
Of London streets, roundabout to the green parks,
The market gardens.

Others wore hard work and honesty
For a Welsh hat; on the strength of those
Went up in the world, never looked back.

A few were immortalised as strawberry sellers.
They smile at us out of rhyme, out of old frames.
Short season—yet the scent of strawberries
Carries an image of pleasure, always in fragrance.

Visiting Light

A single rose-red tile
On an opposite roof
Comes and goes among adjacent slates,
According to light, weather.
Rain, blown off the spring river,
Brings it up proud
Of surrounding greys—
Like an expected face, flushing.

Roofs fascinate—
How they straddle families,
Equal across the too-many
As over the so-lonely,
Giving nothing away.
Discreet above violent stoves,
Cold or much-tumbled beds—
The small saucepan with one furtive egg,
All he can or all he will
Allow himself—which?

Here broods a latent poetry
Nobody reads.
The weed that has managed flowers,
Pinched in a crack,
Lays its thin shadow down
In the afternoons; as the new mother will,
In the room below.

Jackdaws are in these chimneys,
Their difficult lives
Reflect our own; but who will be awake
For the luminous dawn
When the young fly for the first time?

Jackdaws seem inimical
To the mosses, disrupt them down
To me, as I clean my step,
Rubbing with bluestone in the old way.
My scour against the world's indifference
To important symbols—the common roof,
Likeness of patterns.
How warm this moss is,
In my cross hand! A miniscule forest
Full of see-through deaths
That should have had wings. . . .

"Under one roof"
Is such an old expression,
Steady and parental—
Yet life beneath,
Hidden by the roof, changes pace
Daring and malicious as jackdaws,
Unpredictable
As visiting light: or the one rose-red tile
Flushing up—vanishing.

Dysgu

After two months in earphones
We can cope with the mundane
So long as it's slow.
But we're in mined territory:
'Are you near- or far-sighted?'
'I live five minutes away.'

In the coffee-break
Maxwell Sirenya
Reads the overseas news.
An exile from South Africa,
He speaks Welsh
With a Xhosan accent.

Newland, the oldest, remembers

Cycling home alongside
The Glamorganshire Canal
When it was still a canal:
A cone of light moving into dark
And the regular plop of frogs.

Each has his reason to be here
Speaking through declenched teeth:
I'd thought it time to stop
Welshing on the language
And learn about roots,
If only etymological ones.

Daearyddiaeth

The land was always worked.
It was what you lived on.
So the feelings were strong:
The land was in your heart;
The land was underfoot.

It's still farmed, flat and hill,
Some of it good, some bad.
Cash crops may oust *hiraeth*,
But it's still praised: *Gwlad, gwlad*
With the ball hanging air.

And many of the poems
Carry the smack of loam,
In books of earthy style

Whose pages you leaf through
Like someone turning soil.

It wasn't long before
Love and the land were one.
Sweethearts had their contours
While streams grew feminine.
Desire and greening joined.

The genre pullulated.
Venus came on vernal.
The body pastoral
Was sung or lamented
As was Arthur's, grass-graved.

What though of city loves?
Hamlet's country matters
Aren't foreign to the town:
We've enough to ensure
Cupid stays urban.

Poets of the precincts
Lacking parallels
Instinct with the instincts
Should exchange Arcady
For the brick of Cardiff.

Fingers that divagate
Along the vertebrae
Assume Sanquahar Street,
Sesquipedalian
Way to the timber yards.

The gasworks surplus burns
Behind Jonkers Terrace.
Wind flutes and twists the flame,
The gold column broken
Into plaits and tresses.

The path to Thornbury Close
Dwindles into Thornhill
Where tight dawn is seeping
Bit by bit into day:
Someone slowly waking.

One would Think the Deep to be Hoary

For Sebastian Barry

Possible seals disappearing
far out off Pembrokeshire,
sleek commas suddenly lost
in the sea's murky prose,

came back to me (memories
taking a year to surface)
as we returned at midnight
from the Laird and Dog.

It was our daily goal,
two poets retreating
from a Writers' Retreat
to beer's bitter salve.

We'd walk out at twilight
up a drive squeezed through firs
shuttled over by crows
readying for the night

(or once, flung from their nests,
fissile, by a donkey's blaring
Bronx roars through Midlothian
in fractured Trombonese)

and return, talking poetry
in the half-seas-over dark,
down the drive's black on black
curving into deeper dark.

And from poetry, to language:
the world flitched and hung up
in all the different words
in all the different tongues.

Beneath firs weighed by sleeping crows
seal was named in Gaelic—
madra na mara,
the dog of the sea,

while the Welsh one waited,
forgotten and sunk
in the dictionary—
morlo, forlorn *morlo*

only remaining as an image,
greys glint-slicked on distance
and then reclaimed by the sea
bulking in from Ireland.

Seeing them dive again,
ripples bodied through water,
I wondered if they could hear
those unfathomable sounds

of our juke-box favourite,
'Memphis, Tennessee', when Chuck Berry
stretches a guitar string to boom
solid echoes like whales courting.

Dispossessed

Gathered hills bring the sky closer,
stoppering the valley with blue.

Tree ranks on the grassed tips
confuse the sun, corrugating shadow

to display Welsh Office economics:
ten thousand firs for every job.

Yellow bulldozers above Pontygwaith
huff black smoke, sculpting spoil.

Shade-torn light in the main street

suffers the sun's apartheid

and sold-up shops lead to the wreck
of a brewery: *Fernvale—Prince of Ales.*

Starlings congregate on empty chapels
to gloss and bicker the daily lesson.

L.M.C. 1890

Crossing river, road and railway,
I pass the insistent notices:
'This bridge will be closed
if vandalism continues. NCB.'
Beyond the fence,
hundredweight chunks of motor
litter oil-caked earth
as if dropped during a robbery.

On this side of the valley
there are tables in the street,
flutters of bunting
and children eating and playing
to celebrate forty years
of Victory in Europe.
The kids play touch:
'On it. On it. Steve's on it.'

Dead ahead are the two wheels,
one stubborn with green paint

and the other rust-brown
with its cable running
uselessly tight

to the engine-house.
I remember the far wall
and the colliery initials
chiselled high up
above the opening date.
Five more years, I saw,
to another anniversary.

Walking back from Trehafod,
I found a small piece of coal
on the pavement
and it's now on my table:
an inch of memento,
a fossil's miniature strata
smattered with light.

I wonder if I'll still have it
in five years' time
and if I'll remember those kids
running down from the street
to the grassed-over tip
in their toy bowler hats:
plastic crowns brightly coloured
with slices of Union Jack.

Clarinet

Such gravid cloakings
such oaky stains
How can I aged five
connect these solemnities
with the dismembered mechanism
nestling in the purple plush
of its carrying case
or with the spittly reed
fitted to its top
like a yellowed fingernail
And how did my brother Blake
a subscriber to *Meccano Magazine*
become this lone figure in a suit
in the black and white fishbowl
of a live broadcast
from the City Temple Cardiff
Why does the dark music hurt
Who's this Mozart
and why should his movement
be slow

Full Circle

O
so I read
is the only letter
common to all sixty-six
alphabets of the world
Think of it
a baby cries
unswaddled
by circumflex or umlaut
lariats of smoke
from a last cigarette
loop the stop-go talk
of men settling to sleep
on the mattress of the pampas
Oedipus stumbles on
with owl eyes
apostrophizing
Bulgarian onomatopoeia
shares common ground
with Hebraic sweet nothings
and who knows
a nurse might fill in
a toe tag
surname first
and then my initial
without wondering
what it stood for

• CHRIS BENDON •

Constructions

I gaze into Memory, yet
that sheep glows into supernature on the green
that's emerald as ever emeralds.

A dove folds its teleological wings; grips
a tree gripped by ivy
like another Laocöon.

Culture's another genetic game;
like scum on the pond—encoded weeds.
Start or end? Perfectible art?

I descend; to the admonition of the street,
having run without walking, transported.
Yet legs don't seem to need guidance from me;

just keep going, God (*pace* God)
alone knows why. But I construct myself
as I go; for the foreign language of

commonsense.
Someone speaks Welsh. Wales, (whatever that is)
becomes Wales again.

"Apologia pro" Walt Disney

With Cara, caring is a game,
anthropomorphic ruses rule;
I try to fit in her picture page,
we're for Winnie, Flopsy or Mole.
Too pre-verbal for any heuristic purpose,
she pretends to be taken in by
mice in straw bonnets,
sees the tree-house—rightly
as where we live: we, who aren't in
Debrett's or Who's Who,
see parables of domesticity,
warm seven-skinned fantasies
with furry chimerae.

That disowned world, Disneyland:
food, before Freud, thought, or any morality
save—*yes, love, I'm listening*—love.
You yourself were once a cartoon strip;
I reread Enid Blyton and found it good.

But am too tall too old
to fit in that punt
taking blazered animals
through a fluid syntax.

Bob, and Tag, the moral comes clear through:
think, one risky instant,
of the other species' world. . .
Cosy, safe from teeth that do anything
but smile—how to channel the heart's insanity,
the impulse to protect and love to death,
how to care deeply but lightly, lightly
for any creature but the self.
How impossible that is, beyond the page's border,
yet how, now especially, necessary, child.

> As the Wolf might have said
> to Red Riding Hood,

> so diligent, innocent
> so sweet-enough-to-eat.

Swansea

If I could make a poem, as joky, sturdy,
flagrant or encyclopaedic as the streets of this city,
I would.

Secretive too; where is the cathedral?

I can only search high and
low, past Deco cafes, bistros, white Edwardiana
rhetorical against the late sky,
neon strips where life as it can be
is lived vicariously, I vicariously assume,
by insiders
until I come to the close sad streets of
—I almost said home. This, I say,
is where I'd live.

There's the tracks, the fencing
            the historical sea,
all seen through these rows of knowing curtains
qualifying the light of day in rooms entitled,
like volumes: Tredegar, Merlin, Elmwood,
even Timbuktu, Bali Hai;
rooms whose credit's confined to a visitor's stare
and those who live there in a limited way
(apart from grants for glazing or occasional bay windows)
—all too cramped and all in line

but in no guidebook or any known poem
except the obvious rhyme of the streets'
own making, certainly not mine.

I know. I like their squat defiance of logics,
their wit, their litmus tests of love.
And spoke to one who could recall
the night raids of years ago. Walked through
flashback corners of his mind,
streets coming to full stops or piles of bricks.

My mother died in just such a place;
of all ways to go, perhaps the best. Home.

I generalise, quite rightly;
repeat myself in shop windows,
am sunned indulgently.

I change a vowel and then a tense.
At last bump into you, owl-like in your glasses;
—can't understand much, a tourist without a guide.

· INTERVIEW WITH JEREMY HOOKER ·

DL: Could you describe your first involvement with Anglo-Welsh literature?

JH: I went to Wales in 1965, when I became an assistant lecturer at Aberystwyth, University of Wales. It was a one-year appointment but became permanent, so I was there ultimately for seventeen or eighteen years. The first contact I made with an Anglo-Welsh writer, as far as I can remember, was with Roland Mathias, then editor of *The Anglo-Welsh Review*. I met him, we became friends, I did some reviewing for him, and my first "intervention," as it were, in Anglo-Welsh writing, was my review of *The Lilting House*, which came out in 1969—a crucial, pioneering anthology.[1] I wrote a review article of that anthology, one which was very critical of some aspects of contemporary Anglo-Welsh poetry. But instead of making me enemies, it actually made me friends, because I suppose the Anglo-Welsh poets I was criticizing realized that it wasn't malicious and perhaps found some of what I was saying useful. Certainly that was the case with John Tripp, who became a friend. I know the criticism that I made of the poetry he was writing at that time did make a positive difference to him.

So friendships began to, as it were, accumulate. I met Gillian Clarke also around that time, who became a good friend; Roland Mathias, whom I've already mentioned; John Tripp; the late John Ormond; and others. So that was my first intervention, followed by other articles on, for example, Edward Thomas. Then increasingly I was asked to review, especially for *The Anglo-Welsh Review* but also for *Poetry Wales*, then edited by Meic Stephens. I gave lectures on Anglo-Welsh poetry also. Through those first contacts I became quite involved with that generation of Anglo-Welsh writers. I was very interested in and sympathetic towards what a number were doing, and found the range of possibilities within the Anglo-Welsh situation exciting and different for me as an Englishman.

DL: Were you initially asked to write reviews because you brought a different culture to bear, or a different perspective to bear, on Anglo-Welsh literature?

JH: The fact that I was an outsider who was genuinely interested without being patronizing or condescending was welcome. I think also that there wasn't very much criticism of Anglo-Welsh writing at that time. Since then a criticism has arisen, but it's not one of the strengths of the Anglo-Welsh literary scene. Insofar as I was setting up as a critic there was a contribution to be made. There are very good critics within the Anglo-Welsh literary tradition, but they tend to be interpretative, rather than evaluative, and a stronger evaluative criticism is probably something that the poetry could do with.

DL: There still does not seem to be much attention given to Welsh writers by English critics. Perhaps that lack of attention matters less now since there is, finally, a thriving publishing industry and reviewing establishment in Wales. But English critics still seem to resist giving Welsh writers sustained critical attention.

JH: I have felt that, and I still feel it strongly. It's something that the English are blindly cutting themselves off from. Not just Anglo-Welsh writing, from which they could learn, but also Welsh writing in translation. I have said this over and over in different forms, and so in a small way have tried to counter the indifference and to make Welsh and Anglo-Welsh writing a bit better known, through lectures, through talks and, latterly, through writing reviews in *PN Review*. When I write reviews of Anglo-Welsh literature these days I would prefer if possible to do it in an English magazine, so that an English readership has more chance to become aware of what is being and has been done in Wales.

DL: One recent criticism of current Anglo-Welsh poetry is that it draws on or imitates an "international" style, which is confessional, small scale, not sufficiently ambitious in formal or conceptual terms. It's a style associated with much contemporary poetry from the United States.

JH: Yes, but on the other hand I can see among some of the younger Anglo-Welsh positive influences from America. Nigel Jenkins, a poet whose work I particularly respect, has learned quite a lot from the Black Mountain poets and from Gary Snyder. But what you say is true; the confessional mode has certainly influenced a number of poets in Wales, America, England, and elsewhere. In my view, the influence of confessionalism has been mainly baleful because it tends to emphasize ego-experience at the expense of the experience of relationship—different forms of relationship, between the self and the world, the self and the nonself, all kinds of relationships. But that's certainly not the fault—if it is a fault—of Anglo-Welsh poetry.

DL: Do you think that the elder sibling relationship of Welsh literature to Anglo-Welsh literature has been detrimental or positive, or some of both?

JH: I think it's been very positive. I probably have an argument here with somebody like John Barnie, who marks the difference between the Welsh and the Anglo-Welsh and tends to lump the Anglo-Welsh with the English. In my view the borderline which the poets cross, and they often do cross it of course, is in their own minds and bodies. The person who is writing in English is in fact Welsh and in some instances a Welsh speaker. But I think that those borderers, as I call them, are in a situation with exciting possibility. This isn't to deny that a sense of division or fragmentation, or difficulty of integration, cannot be considerably painful. But at the same time I think that tensions can be very positive and have proved to be, and the Anglo-Welsh poets that interest me most are those who have been most open to Welsh influences. I think for example of Tony Conran—much undervalued, a powerful and inventive poet who is certainly fetching some of his power, some of his inventiveness, from his knowledge of Welsh. In a very different way Roland Mathias has drawn strongly throughout his writing upon his Welsh nonconformist roots. Then there's novelist Emyr Humphreys, who is also a fine poet and who has made important literature out of the bordering situation.

DL: Perhaps the stronger Anglo-Welsh poets have allowed the Welsh background to draw them through to cultural, literary, and historical material not available to other English-language poets. But wouldn't this be a problem for weaker poets who might then feel a need to "prove" Welshness in order to publish?

JH: During the sixties and seventies, when I was living in Wales, there was quite a lot of very self-conscious poetry: "I'm proving myself to be Welsh," or on the other hand, "I'm a wretch who is unworthy to claim to be Welsh." At the same time there was lots of anti-English rhetoric, at a rather superficial level antagonistic to tourism. There were recognizable kinds of poems that tended to produce weak writing, which arose directly out of the Anglo-Welsh situation. And one could do with far less of that.

DL: Does the Garlick/Mathias *Anglo-Welsh Poetry 1480-1980* anthology present a usable tradition for Anglo-Welsh poets?[2]

JH: It has proved so for some writers. There is proof of that in, for example, the poetry of Raymond Garlick himself, who of course is one of the discoverers, or if you like, founders, of that tradition. Looking at that particular anthology, yes, there are interesting poems before the twentieth century that can be described as "Anglo-Welsh." But much as I respect the scholarship and historical knowledge of Roland Mathias and Raymond Garlick, I am among those who think that it's really only in this century that a recognizable Anglo-Welsh tradition arises. This is argued by Glyn Jones, if I recall correctly, in his important book, *The Dragon Has Two Tongues.* He makes quite clear the social and historical conditions that have produced the Anglo-Welsh writer in the twentieth century.

DL: It's still a live debate. It could be the kind of debate which—whatever the merits of the argument—will produce good work by causing poets to think about identity, tradition, and connections to the past.

JH: That's a very good point because irrespective of certain instances of historical truth, a poet's interpretation of an historical situation, even if historically erroneous, even if the poet is being a myth-maker—as I think David Jones is quite often in his view of Welsh history—can produce good work. Another figure who's been tremendously important to me—and still is—is John Cowper Powys, whom I've written about.[3] There's an instance of a man who virtually turned himself into a Welshman, and he's not the only example of that. A number of the writers whom we've talked about were not Welsh by birth but chose to become Welsh. I have friends who are as English as I am by ancestry and origin but who identify themselves as Welsh because they find in the Welsh tradition something that was lacking in the English.

It's partly the cultural continuity, the possibility of integration, and the religious dimension that goes along with that, whether it's vague or more specific.

John Cowper Powys is for me one of the great archetypal examples. He did have some Welsh ancestry, but like most of the modernists, his life was a process of self-making. T. S. Eliot made himself into an Englishman. Ezra Pound made himself into a European. They were all making themselves into something or other because they felt there was no existing culture that they could step into and identify with. So they had to remake themselves, and this, I think, is what some English and other people have done by identifying with the Welsh.

DL: For a number of years women have been very poorly represented in magazines and anthologies, in *Ten Anglo-Welsh Poets* and so forth.[4] Then, quite suddenly there has been an explosion of very fine poetry from women writers in Wales. What is it about their poetry that you think is working well?

JH: In recent years, I've been particularly interested in poetry by women, and I think that some of the most powerful poetry coming from the Anglo-Welsh poets as well as from elsewhere is by women. I've recently given a lecture called "Taliesin's Daughters," which I will ultimately publish. I'm there considering the work of several contemporary Welsh women poets writing in English. The poets with whom I'm specifically concerned are Gillian Clarke, Ruth Bidgood, Hilary Llewellyn-Williams, Christine Evans, and Jean Earle. It's not to say those are the only women poets from Wales that I read with interest and pleasure, but those are the ones I focus upon. As the title of the talk indicates, I am arguing that the Taliesin tradition, which is in a nutshell the ability to get outside oneself and inhabit imaginatively some other being or form of life—is a tradition which recently women poets in Wales have adopted. I thought that Christine Evans's most recent book, *Cometary Phases* had in it some very powerful poems. There's one in particular called, I believe, "Whale's Song," in which she is identifying imaginatively with the whale. That's a fine example of what I mean by the ability to get beyond the self, to use empathy. Without getting into sexual politics, all I'll say is that is a gift. Women poets seem to have access to something that most, if not all, male poets are cut off from, whether necessarily or for ideological reasons of cultural conditioning. In my view, not enough male poets have followed this exciting imaginative direction.

DL: The publishing outlets in Wales now seem especially encouraging to women writers.

JH: Yes. Of course so much is owed to *Poetry Wales*, Seren Books, Roland Mathias, and others.[5] When I first went to Wales this situation didn't exist. It wasn't possible for poets to get together bodies of work because there weren't publishers for that work in Wales. But now you have the spectacle of young poets, Robert Minhinnick, for example, or John Davies, who are producing collections of poems every two or three or four years. That's not in all instances a good thing: a poet can always publish too much. But on the other hand, it's a much better situation than manuscripts accumulating.

DL: In one of your essays in *The Presence of the Past* you argue that much Anglo-Welsh poetry is a poetry of memory.[6] But can't memory as a subject or focus play out after a while?

JH: A poetry in which the poet has no more than his or her own ego to fall back upon is quickly exhausted and has in any case certain in-built limitations, which isn't to say that some of the important poetry of the past doesn't come out of personal experience—of course it does. But in my view it usually comes from personal experience that relates to some sense of order outside the self, whether that is a cosmic or religious order, or a social order, or a sense of historical order, or whatever it may be—something that the individual mind feels it can participate in. There, I think, is where the poetry of memory fits in.

DL: Could you define the term more fully?

JH: By "poetry of memory" I mean not only memory of one's own past, though that is important. Each individual has a sense of personal being through continuity, from having been the child or the young adult having lived a continuous life. It's very dangerous, psychologically, for any of us to get cut off from our own personal lives. But I think it's equally undesirable and dangerous to get cut off from our familial and ancestral past. And for this one doesn't have to look only at the Welsh and Anglo-Welsh writers; this is true of American writers whom I admire greatly: Toni Morrison talks very eloquently about the "danger of killing the ancestor." I think that by and large, the Welsh and the Anglo-Welsh have sought not only not to kill the ancestor but to give the ancestor a continuing life in poetry. Roland Mathias, for example, is a poet powerfully affected by the nonconformist conscience. In his poetry, that makes him continually compare himself with his ancestors and find himself wanting. The result is, among other things, a powerfully moral poetry.

But a poetry of memory can work in many other ways as well. One of the things one notices about Welsh poetry (which to me, unfortunately, is available only in translation) is that from the historical Taliesin to the present it has emphasized brotherhood, and increasingly with women poets in our century, sisterhood. In the nineteenth century this spirit is more or less democratic and liberal, but if you go back into the Middle Ages and beyond, then it's tribal. Nevertheless, it is the same spirit, a spirit of community, that's manifesting itself at different times during the long historical life of this culture. And that is one of the things I feel that the living Welsh and Anglo-Welsh poet can have access to.

DL: That would argue against John Barnie's position that there is little difference formally or materially between the English and Anglo-Welsh poet.

JH: But John Barnie came to live in Wales later than I did. Back in the 1960s the ideas that you and I have been talking about were very vital, and although I think they still are vital in some quarters, there is also a new spirit abroad among some Anglo-Welsh poets that tends to bear out John Barnie's argument. There are undoubtedly poets following ambitions that are indistinguishable, really, from Anglo-American literary ambitions generally. We know what that means if we've read the correspondence of Robert Frost and see that terrible, personal need for, hunger for, recognition that results in competitiveness, that inflates the ego to some enormous size—and, well, Anglo-Welsh poets are like any other people.

In the present generation we do have poets like Nigel Jenkins, Christine Evans, Gillian Clarke, and others who are reaching out to a world beyond themselves, which they nevertheless belong to. You also have others who are indistinguishable from the Anglo-American confessional tradition. Tony Conran is the best critic of this kind of thing. One thing that he identifies in the English poetic tradition in the twentieth century is—I can't quote exactly, but something like—"the production of personal experience as a kind of commodity." That's what the poem has become. There's more than one grain of uncomfortable truth in what he says, and it can be applied to some Anglo-Welsh poets.

DL: There does seem to be a significant amount of promotional work done on behalf of Anglo-Welsh poetry—an attempt to "sell" the idea of an Anglo-Welsh literature and tradition. Or to put it positively, a desire to establish an Anglo-Welsh audience by working the poetry into school curricula, setting up public readings, and so forth.

JH: It's interesting to me that you should put those two movements together, and I can see exactly what you mean. But I think it was a bit different during the period that I was living in Wales. I gave a talk at one time, published in *The Presence of the Past*, which is about Anglo-Welsh poetry in the sixties but also looked at some work published in the seventies. Later I wrote a piece on the young Anglo-Welsh poets. There are points of continuity. There's also been a great change. And no doubt, given the present situation, there will be further changes. The example of Tony Conran, Roland Mathias, David Jones, and others show one direction with exciting possibilities. But there's another direction altogether which is more self-promotional, and that also can, I suppose, be identified with Anglo-Welshness. I think it would be a great pity if that were to become dominant.

DL: How central is a religious dimension to Anglo-Welsh literature?

JH: I've written increasingly about the religious dimension in conjunction with the historical and the cultural in recent years, and it's quite clear that one of the differences between Welsh and Anglo-Welsh, and English and American poetry is in their religious preoccupations. I usually find that I very soon have to introduce the word "religious" when talking about the poetry of, say, John Ormond, Gillian Clarke, or Alun Lewis, or that of writers who have a specific commitment, like Emyr Humphreys, Roland Mathias, or David Jones. One doesn't want to label people religious who would resist the labeling. But having said that, the religious impulse is very strong and very much alive in quite a lot of the work of the writers that you and I have talked about. And, generally, less in the English or American.

DL: One thing you didn't mention in going through some of the characteristics of Anglo-Welsh writing is the political dimension, which was and to an extent still is in the forefront of much Anglo-Welsh writing, good and bad.

JH: One had to be very much aware of politics during the years that I was living in Wales. The Welsh are a very political people, and they live in a very political situation. In broad terms their politics is mainly democratic, with which on the whole I identify. So in some respects I was much happier with the politics of Wales than I was with the politics of my own country. And also I have considerable sympathy with Welsh nationalism. Perhaps partly as a result of middle age, but also I think because of the world situation, my politics are less sure and much less dogmatic than they have been at any other point of my life. I'm more aware now that there is something in most poets that is inherently conservative. I'm equally very keen to separate that entirely from conservatism as it's used in contemporary politics—the Tories, Thatcherism—which is not conservative but something that actually cuts us off from or identifies very narrowly with certain ideals of the past. Having said that, yes, I'm sympathetic towards the basic democratic ideals dominant in Wales. And, yes, it marks the poetry of this whole period.

DL: During the sixties and seventies, Welsh nationalism almost seems to have been obligatory for a generation of poets.

JH: It was for that generation of poets who were really shaken by the referendum, to the point where some actually stopped writing, at least for a period.[7] Others changed direction. They didn't know what to do. I think now perhaps the shock of that has been got over and there is a sense of new possibilities. But certainly throughout the time that I was in Wales, it was almost obligatory for an Anglo-Welsh poet to be a Welsh nationalist, which isn't to impugn the authenticity of what it was and is: completely genuine. Sometimes it produced good political poetry and sometimes it produced bad political poetry.

DL: Has politics become less important to the younger generation of English-language poets in Wales?

JH: There are political poets among the younger generation of course, like Mike Jenkins and Nigel Jenkins. But the situation has changed by and large, and perhaps there are certain things that this younger generation feels that it can take for granted. I think that between literary generations there's always the desire to kill the father. And it's difficult to recognize what one owes to the father. It's clear to me that the younger Anglo-Welsh poets do owe something important to the founding fathers.

It's rather surprising looking back that the one word we haven't used as far as I can recall is "praise." Welsh and Anglo-Welsh poetry is really a praise poetry. And I respond to that very positively because by and large, with some exceptions, poetry in English isn't. And there are reasons why it's very difficult at this point in the twentieth century to write praise poetry—the destructive reality we inhabit, and so on. But one of my own fundamental impulses is to praise, and the ability to do that is present in the Welsh and the Anglo-Welsh poetry, and I learned from that and obtained support from that.

• CHRISTINE EVANS •

Small Rain

May 1986: after Chernobyl

For weeks the wind strained from the east
So ground and air were dry with a touch of steel
the sky's face pursed, indomitable, blank.

Close in the pod of our own concerns
we have reached the nunnery scene
when the first rain sighs and draws our gaze.

I remember teaching them rain-as-symbol:
fertility, wholeness, healing, grace.
Larkin's arrow-shower. Heart's-ease of tears.

This falls so gently on dust-stiffened green
new leaves and blossom that we've waited for

we open windows to its breath—and hear
a million small mouths suck and whisper.

I used to dream of dancing in the rain
with nothing on, Rhiannon confides,
and no-one titters, we nod and understand

a dozen women, eleven with their lives
unfolding, held still and curious as cattle
by rain in Wales! We gaze and go on gazing

as though not one of us had realised
the world could go on glistening
poisoned. The lesson falters; goes on

but I am seeing each of these grave girls
as a kind of ark, and Ararat
a point in time we have to hope to find

and listening to our futures being fed.

Whale Dream

In a dream I loosed my voice
into the echoing vault of the ocean
knowing once it would have stirred an answer
half a world away among the ice.

Slowed and strengthened to cetacean pulse
I swam in the womb of the world

and the stars were a whalespine above me
charged focuses that sang my bearings

and I could read the streams with all the skin
of my glistening long body
and let the breath flow through me in a song
serene but reaching, the refrain of journeys

going on means going far
going far means returning

and as a dolphin sleeps with half of its brain
so half of me knew I was a woman
dreaming a whale; for the rest I seemed
a cetacean's fear of being human

shrivelled back to sharps
and bulges, skin cracked and tight
over jerky bones, skull full of hooks
grinning their way to the light

while I was richly lined and supple,
the water curved me like a lover
stroked at every creaming touch
whirlpools of colour down my flanks.

We smile with our whole bodies
we see where all is dark
we hear where all is still:
water heals itself of spaces

But my singing was a memory of how
nursed deep within the waves' turmoil
in the still heart of flowing
we wove our patterns of shared song

in a language kinder than words
loops and swirls of sense that make words seem
small closed hooks
to button meaning, keep it closed.

In images that shone against the dark
more immediate than tasting
more shifting than pictures
pulsing on the nerves like touch

I was charged with hymns to water, and in praise
of the sun-bred krill; hunting chants of the tribes
who ride an adrenalin frenzy;
Blue Whale meditations

and the Humpback sagas—of the First Men
and the one lost boy;
the heroes of the Hundred Savings
when sea took back the land;

and shared the disappointment of the dolphins
when they first leapt to meet
the new vibrations, thinking them
a language they could learn to answer

and added my cries
to echoes from the Inland Sea

when, twice, it boiled and white heat leapt
in waves back to the sky

and in shadow memory was urged
towards the bay off Iki island
where one porpoise under torture
drew two thousand to let blood

and saw far flickered messages
from sisters swimming under other suns
until in their ingenious deaf haste
men clogged that channel too

and when the sense of man sighed through me
I sent out only sorrow: he must move
in inner darkness, strung with pain.
How scarred he is, how young.

To sing is to join
the song of the universe
is fullness and emptiness
beginning and end

But knowing there were so few left
to sing, to remember
I heard the colours of my notes grow tender
for the long-prehuman clearness.

My journey was ending. I could taste
the poison in the water and I knew

the baby stored far down above my tail
would not be born, my blood would use him.

When we meet in the depths
I sang, *there will be leaping*
bodies matching as minds do
as stars and darkness in that deeper ocean

though I felt only exhaustion
fear in an oily tide
and anger like white flashes
spreading outwards from the land

Of our coming is no trace
in our leaving is no goal
formlessness is the sum
of the singing of all things

All over the world, every year
whales have woven new strands in their song.
I woke sensing the last one
was what I had lost.

Power

1

My wing-tips finger the early stars.
They shiver at my voice.

I swivel my head to churn the still-green shadows;
Listen as they sink back into pattern:

Hear the twitch of a mouse
The tap of a beetle, the whisper of fur
On a body slung between mothwings.
The zigzag staccato of the pipistrelle.

Feel the whirlpool in each eye
Begin to suck and deepen,
Tugging darkness from its bones.

My mind flexes and the world
Breathes like panic, hiding.

Each nerve foams with prompting.
My feathers quicken and lift.
The deep roots of my primaries
Thrum and quiver
                    Let go
And the ground falls from me.
At first I move soft as mist
Drift light as a dandelion clock
Down the valley

But the cave in my brain
Rings with small cries, the clench
And shudder of flesh, its warm
Red weight.

I come over the fields like the wind
Scooping darkness, threshing the sky.

2

My blood is blue-black
my head studded with eyes.
Inside the cradle of my legs
I carry hunger.

Since first frost I slept
in the curl of a yellow bramble leaf;
in a blazing instant
woke in the sun to spin my claim
paying out silk like blood or song
moving in a dance
the ancestors inside my head
crooned for me

working purpose to a mesh of clots
watching them become invisible
as the sun swam higher
feeling the spokes begin to thresh and turn
waiting
shrinking my will to a small red glow
keeping my mind still as a pool
under dark trees
waiting.
The hub of my life is hunger.

When the tremor in the air means meat
the hairs on my legs will stiffen and quiver
a whole body tingling
will lift me and launch me;

I will tilt the slack sack of my body
and finger my way down.

The wide gape of my legs
longs to enfold and mould what is mine
soothe its spasms in a shroud of silk
stroke it into succulence
love it until it is all juice.

I grow huge and glaring; begin to advance.

Llŷn

Skies tower here, and we are small.

Winters, we sleep on a flap of land
in a dark, salt throat.
Huge cold breaths of wind and rain
hurtle over, cascade down
till we feel the house hunch.

Along the northern edge, the rocks
go on holding on
but tamed by the ice, the pale clays
of the southern shore slide under.

When morning comes at last
houses sit up with pricked ears
on reefs of land the black tide
leaves, or sidle crab-wise

to the lane, their small squashed faces
giving nothing of their thoughts away.

In summer, flowers loosening with seed
reach out to fingerstroke
cars passing in the long sweet dusk.
Hay-meadows sigh. Pearl-pale
in the bracken on the headland
shorn ewes step delicately
wary as young unicorns.

The sea we look out over is a navel
the wrinkled belly-button
of an older world: after dark
like busy star-systems, the lights
of Harlech, Aberystwyth, Abergwaun
wink and beckon. The sun's gone down
red as a wound behind Wicklow.
A creaking of sail away
Cernyw and Llydaw wait.

Once, here was where what mattered
happened. A small place
at the foot of cliffs of falling light;
horizons that look empty.
If we let ourselves believe it,
fringes.

Second Language

For Carys P., Carys T., Elena, Manon, Nia, and Teyrnon

I watch their faces rise to meet me
from the green depths of a culture
older than I can fathom. They glide
as if weighted by dreams or water

through my lessons, taking notes,
assiduously handing in assignments
in good time, browsing gravely
through all the books I offer, *thanking* me—

and all the time I feel I could be
beguiling selkie people to the land
to the bright amnesiac desert air
where I burn off my life without blossoming.

Five girls and a boy riding a name out of myth
whose language fills the mouth like fruit
who have grown in the delicate light
of an old walled garden that was once the world.

Manon, whom I see in jet and amber
accepting tribute, was the first
tangled in the word-lures, drawn out
to stand beside me with her colours brittling.

She claims she heard no echoes, never sang
in her own language. Now the others hover
offering in devout, tentative palms

iridescence from the inside of their minds.

In their calm faces I can find no clues
that they are still at ease in their own skins
that dredging for this voice has drowned no other
and my teaching has not made them strangers.

▪ TONY CONRAN ▪

Giants

A castle is a wedge in the soul.

He had purchase from it,
Leverage
Like a pair of forks back to back
To divide
The warm belonging root of us.

I climb now to the Earl's opposite.

▪

Up the sharp scree, up the lace alb
Of the hill, stepping
Where disks of rhyolite chink,
Up to the bleached skeleton

Of a hill-fort, laid out
On a limb of Yr Eifl
Under the running cloud.

Tre'r Ceiri we call it, town of giants.

Really, the giants are us,
Denizens larger than life
Of the erected scree. While we live
Each of these cauldrons of dry stone
Is capped like a kraal. Smoke
Twists its way through birch bark.
Moans of oxen hang round us like mist.

While we live, these parapets stand.

Counting Song

In the soul. But first, in the soil.

Destructible wood and stone
Of the castle-builders. Lands
By compulsory purchase
(Or otherwise) appropriated
To service castles. Monasteries
By the grace of God
Moved up river. Whole townlands
Picked, dusted and re-potted
The other end of the world.

In the soil. But second, in the coffers.

Destructible writs, great seals
Dangling. Sheriffs,
Law-courts, officers
For the registration of fair
Trading. The quiet ways
Of simony and graft. The King's Peace
Stealing in on you
Like a mist over water-meadows.

In the coffers. But third, in the belly.

In the belly of compassion
The children hungry. In the belly
Of anger, fat cats of the King.
Destructible devils
Out of the corner of eyes.

In the belly. But fourth, in the prophecies.

Caernarfon Across Brown Fields

This is where empire begins.
It's the dragon's tooth.

Polygonal towers, faces
Of vertical shadow and light
Like long gem-crystals.

Patterning of tower and wall

With bands of coloured stone.

Three stone eagles face the sea.

—Such walls, such towers
Curtain under the eagles
Byzantium the Second Rome . . .

And whose idea was it, grubbing up
Tubers of a third
To sprout in these hills?
Which *Wledig*, Macsen or Cystennin,
Caesar Longshanks, plaudited
Imperator of the Brits . . .

Empire. That's what
Bites into these brown fields,
Rears over the trees
Into white air. Who set it
Ticking away like a bomb
Weeks, years, millennia?

Gwales

By the westerly tump of Gwales
A dead skull, a door, a castle.
    The three ravens will fly.

By the South Gut, at the inlet,
A live eye, a tower, a window.
    The three ravens will fly.

A dead skull, a door, a castle
Mined by puffins, gobble of gannets.
The three ravens will fly.

A live eye, a tower, a window
Between drifting gannets, white as blizzard.
The three ravens will fly.

Mined by puffins, gobble of gannets,
Civilization crowds and crashes.
The three ravens will fly.

Between drifting gannets, white as blizzard,
Red dereliction fastens on wishes.
The three ravens will fly.

Civilization crowds and crashes.
Nine ages bleed on Bosworth meadow.
The three ravens will fly.

Red dereliction fastens on wishes—
A dead skull under the tump of Britain.
The three ravens will fly.

Wild Form

For the wedding of Ellie and Steve

That's not a hydrangea, is it?
Yes, the wild form—
A floating raft of tiny pink
Peppercorns

And round it, like winds on a compass,
Huge sterile
Florets, velvet and crinoline
Like a waxwork smile.

It is the peppercorn buds mean business—
The real flowers,
Symmetrically accurate
Jabs of power.

Stamens prod out like the knobs
Of the Red Queen's crown.
They are the naked thing. Bees
Crowd down

To a consummation of damp pollen,
The bloom's
Orgasmic cry of colour
In a green room.

Elegy For The Welsh Dead, in the Falkland Islands, 1982

Gŵyr a aeth Gatraeth oedd ffraeth eu llu.
Glasfedd eu hancwyn, a gwenwyn fu.
—Y Gododdin (sixth century)

(Men went to Catraeth, keen was their company.
They were fed on fresh mead, and it proved poison.)

Men went to Catraeth. The luxury liner

For three weeks feasted them.

They remembered easy ovations,

Our boys, splendid in courage.

For three weeks the albatross roads,

Passwords of dolphin and petrel,

Practised their obedience

Where the killer whales gathered,

Where the monotonous seas yelped.

Though they went to church with their standards

Raw death has them garnished.

Men went to Catraeth. The Malvinas

Of their destiny greeted them strangely.

Instead of affection there was coldness,

Splintering iron and the icy sea,

Mud and the wind's malevolent satire.

They stood nonplussed in the bomb's indictment.

Malcolm Wigley of Connah's Quay. Did his helm

Ride high in the war-line?

Did he drink enough mead for that journey?

The desolated shores of Tegeingl,
Did they pig this steel that destroyed him?
The Dee runs silent beside empty foundries.
The way of the wind and the rain is adamant.

Clifford Elley of Pontypridd. Doubtless he feasted.
He went to Catraeth with a bold heart.
He was used to valleys. The shadow held him.
The staff and the fasces of tribunes betrayed him.
With the oil of our virtue we have annointed
His head, in the presence of foes.

Phillip Sweet of Cwmbach. Was he shy before girls?
He exposes himself now to the hags, the glance
Of the loose-fleshed whores, the deaths
That congregate like gulls on garbage.
His sword flashed in the wastes of nightmare.

Russell Carlisle of Rhuthun. Men of the North
Mourn Rheged's son in the castellated vale.
His nodding charger neighed for the battle.
Uplifted hooves pawed at the lightning.
Now he lies down. Under the air he is dead.

Men went to Catraeth. Of the forty-three
Certainly Tony Jones of Carmarthen was brave.
What did it matter, steel in the heart?
Shrapnel is faithful now. His shroud is frost.

With the dawn men went. Those forty-three,
Gentlemen all, from the streets and byways of Wales,

Dragons of Aberdare, Denbigh and Neath—
Figment of empire, whore's honour, held them.
Forty-three at Catraeth died for our dregs.

• RUTH BIDGOOD •

Kindred

I am still a mile or two
from the source. In spite of myself
I hear the stony flow of the stream
as speech, though not about anything
I know. No bleating, no bird-call;
the only other sound is a breeze
over molinia-grass. It is hard
not to think of a sigh.

On either hand the shallow slope
of the bank steepens, further up,
to a low hill; behind that
rises high land. Nothing seems to grow
for miles but long pale grass
in ankle-turning clumps. My mind

sees little horns of moss on the moors,
cups of lichen on grey rocks,
red-green of whinberry leaves.

Round the next curve of the stream
low broken walls delineate a life
almost beyond my imagining.
Something calls, with a voice
seeming at first as alien
as the stream's, yet inescapable,
and after a while more like
the calling of kindred,
or my own voice echoing
from a far-off encompassing wall.

Gale

The gale has flung great branches
to lie in pools; it has not finished yet.
Through wind and rain there comes
a whistling and a maniacal whooping,
a stamping, a rushing.

Six dripping sheep dart by,
mad-eyed: then two draggled dogs,
swift, low to the ground: then,
thudding past on his pony, a tall man,
sodden hat drooping to his eyes,
his shouts as violent as the day.

Above the road, grazing sheep
catch the terror and run into
a jigging pattern of pushing heads
and grey wet curly backs.

Suddenly it is over, the pony
and the stragglers gone chasing down the road,
the whooping and the whistling gone.
The flock, quiet, dip heads to grass.

Everything feels almost safe,
except that in the wet gale's boom and yowl
fear still sometimes finds a voice
as it has done all day.

Banquet

At the time of the nineteenth-century religious revivals it was said of two old
North Breconshire women, "The Revival was a banquet for them."

Their youth was poor and barren as the land.
The mould that should have formed them women
held some flaw, broke early,
spilling them out to harden into things
men's eyes would never rest on
except with scorn.
                    They were strong, though.
Fighting their stony patch
on its shelf of rock, they won.
The mound-encircled garden was rough, plain,
growing food, not flowers; yet as they touched
the juicy crispness of new sap-filled leaves
they learned a kind of tenderness.

By rushlight at the dark of the year,
when knitting-pins made winter music,
they could remember those great skies
spread lordly-wise above them when they wandered
hill-pastures, scratting grey tough wool
from fence and thorn.

Year after year

came back thaw, singing, airy softness,
pulsing of the blood, to tease and mock,
then gale and fall of leaf and snow
to tell them what they knew too well.

Then, when they were almost old, he came.
He preached in the river-meadow
to crowds who wept and begged and leapt,
cried 'Glory, glory!', fell
foaming on the rough tussocks of grass.
He seemed to speak softly, yet from the hill
they heard, and from their hut came
fearfully, like unhandled ponies.
He looked up, smiled. They were unused to love.
This thing seemed other than the rut and musk
most knew (not they). Stumbling,
each clutching the other on the sliding stones,
they took the short cut down.

That was the start of it—their banqueting-time,
wine of God, and gold, and bath
of sweetest milk, damask tent
and bed of silk, lemon-grove,
low-hung moon, summer, subtle song,

their rest, their dawn, their piercing love.

The dark time came again. They rattled logs
into flame, and shadows walked the wall.
They grew old, hunched over the hearth.
One muttered words he taught,
the other joined her in her prayer,
catching at the rags of a memory. Snow
sifted under the door. Each stretched her hands
to the fire, like a beggar,
and waited for the placing in her palm
of a small dole of love.

Image

At the head of the lead-mine valley
above sliding stone is grass, above grass
a track, a hundred yards or so
of old wide rutted thoroughfare
crossing, high up, the valley's line,
starting abruptly, climbing
to a sudden end in tussocky slush.

It is this you are giving me
as an image of living, this short
lonely road with its traces
of ancient use, its purposeful climbing
and awesome views, this road
coming from nowhere, ending in nothing—
a bleaker symbol than the sparrow
flying through light from dark to dark.

I believe in origins
and destinations, but am hard put
to define this road's whole journey.
You are unimpressed by my tale
of a lost map, want to see and touch
the wounds of the land. I think
somewhere the slope's rough pelt must bear
the cicatrice of a continuing path.

You have a sceptical eye for the blank hill.
You do not feel an onwardness
in the ancient road. Yet in evening sun
you have come to sit beside it, far above
old spoil-heaps and the rusty markers
of black shafts, to watch how line on line
the multiple horizon rears its dark
against red sun, to hear how pure
is the voice of the poisoned stream.

Speech

The caravan is hidden in the trees
on the hillside. On the open slope
washing flies boldly in the rain.
Linen still scatters drops
after the shower has passed upstream.
The dark valley is inarticulate.
It strives towards an answer
for the growing sun, utters
half-formed words in a glow on the crags,

a gleam on the river. Sunlight
rushes along the hill, wakes the line's colour
to clear pert sentences. There they are,
red tablecloth, striped sheets, pyjamas,
gaudy apron, flamboyant and ridiculous,
halfway up a mountain, shouting unabashed
their jolly clichés, giving by accident
to the superb and half-dumb desolation
a transient, trivial, cheerful speech.

Llanfihangel

Some still remember the rose-window
shining through dusk, the bells
that played hymn-tunes, the one
that tolled for the valley's dead.
Splendid Victorian folly, the church itself
lived less than a century. Soft stone
sopped up the endless rain. Above cross-point
of nave and transept, heavy tower
made an infinitesimal shift, chancel arch
moved a millimetre out of true.
In the pulpit, an intermittent drip
punctuated sermons. Whisper by whisper
flaking began, softest of plaster-fall
from pillar and wall, drift of dust
on chaliced wine. Then as a doomed mind,
whose tiny eccentricities have given
little unease, suddenly lurches to grosser
irrationality, the building shed

a first sodden chunk of facing-stone,

and was put away.

Damp barricaded silence lasted

till the slow thudding months of demolition,

the final blasting of the tower.

Grass, yew-trees, graves remain,

and in a few old minds regret

no longer sharp, but steady as rain

that brought down stone and fed the flood of grass.

The Hook

1

I named it sickle. But he
uses it, the old man, and he called it:
the hook.

No longer new; a flatter curve
of blade than the gold on red: crescent
of an ellipse;

and implement, not emblem:
dull, rust oiled with usage; nicked, the
harshened silver edge.

But a tool perfects, almost
like nature, more stringent than art: millenia
winnowed to this

shape since Egypt was
the world's grainhouse, longer:
a moon-edge

cutting finer than a straight:
grass, not flesh: only the point would embed,
opening an enemy

like a full sack, or the edge hack
a limb, the swung fist past its mark;
but savage enough

a symbol of agronomy
for rising serfs. The crossed hammer beat
this out blue once

in a man's fist; but mass
produced now for a dwindling few, this tool,
this weapon:

the steel flattened, arched, made
keen, even the white ash turned smooth, and
ferruled, by machine.

But finely weighted, this one:
light, as if I hefted only a handle, even
to the left hand,

even as it learns the backsweep.
I stooped and swung; the wristy, ambidextral hook
slew grass,

forestroke and back. I think
no eye bought this, but wrist: by balanced weight,
like grain;

and that it is beautiful only
now, for the coarse use that refined it,
like the sea-stone.

2

Beautiful too is the word:
swathe. I laid low all afternoon tall, green,
slender seeded grasses

of more elegance than poplars.
Their stems fell sheaved after the stroke
like armfuls of bluebells,

the blade was wet with sap.
Doubled I stooped, climbing the field
all the hot afternoon

for these red stigmata,
skinned blisters on the mounts of
both white palms.

Ramsey Island

Drab gorse crouches;
and the stunted thorn, its back bent
from the lash, fleeing
the wind—
but root-bound,
like the girl becoming laurel.

There are no nymphs or gods pursuant
here;
barely a crippled tree is bared
against the sky.

Only wind, running
the turf one way like a close pelt;
and precipices to the sea.

Even men, who root anywhere,
landed, lasted a few brute seasons out,
were gone.
There is nothing to grip on.

■

The island's a bird sanctuary now.
Like the leaning wind, it has
prevailed,
becoming finally what it always was.

The once-gutted stone

habitation has been renovated for the warden.
With his deep-freeze, radio and books,
his sinecure's
as steady as a lighthouse job.

He'll last here longer than those
who had to, and couldn't—
each crude, repetitive meal
earned
singly, eaten
after darkness off the day's bare plate—

the fish-taste of gull-eggs;
a rim of chipped bone.

▪

Cut off in winter
for weeks at a stretch, you hunched to stare across
the straits and see
a man ploughing a field dark
on the mainland in a cloud of gulls,
as if on the next hill.

Here the dirt was
thinner than the scalp on your skull.

But there were worse straits—
the rock was
fast;
you thought of those out in that running sea.

A fine day
was not a respite but increase of labour.

Yet there were the moments: going
out at morning;
the sea sometimes, when the back straightened.

In a bleak, intermittent
diary, kept a full year he survived
on the island, Ivor Arnold, poor
at spelling, and grudging
his entries
like flour or paraffin or twine,
recorded of a day in March, 1908:

'Wind S. A fine day. I could hear
Will Morris Pencarnan talking
to his horses yesterday from Congrwn Bach.'

Living

Living touches us
strangely, as if with accidental
sadness:
       an old woman
buying a single onion
at a stall;
         the rust-frail
edge of corrugated-iron sheeting
and a mattress

disembowelled on a stretch
of waste ground;

                      and
in the night a high, white moon
like a coin
from which the face is worn.

                             I record

these
facts beyond other comment,
only because it might be as if
they never were.

Summer 1984

Summer of strike and drought,
of miners' pickets standing on blond verges,
of food parcels and

hosepipe bans . . . And as (or so
the newspapers reported it) five rainless
months somewhere disclosed

an archaeology of long-evicted
dwellings on a valley-floor, the reservoir
which drowned them

having slowly shrunk towards
a pond between crazed banks, the silted
houses still erect,

even, apparently, a dusty
bridge of stone you might still walk
across revealed intact

in that dry air, a thing not seen
for years; just so (though this the papers
did not say)

the weeks and months of strike saw
slowly and concurrently emerge in shabby
river-valleys in South Wales

—in Yorkshire too, and Durham,
Kent and Ayrshire—villages no longer
aggregates of dwellings

privatised by television, but
communities again, the rented videos and tapes
back in the shop,

fridge-freezers going back
—so little to put in them, anyway—and
meetings, meetings in their place,

in workmen's clubs and miners' welfare
halls, just as it had been once, communities
beleaguered but the closer,

the intenser for it, with resources
now distributed to need, and organised to last,
the dancefloors stacked

with foodstuffs like a dockside, as if
an atavistic common memory, an inheritance
perhaps long thought romantic,

like the old men's proud and bitter
tales of 1926, was now being learnt again,
in grandchildren and

great-grandchildren of their bloodline:
a defiance and a unity which even sixty years
of almost being discounted never broke.

· JOHN BARNIE ·

Optional

The bull is crystallized out of the black byre
In thermals of body heat and the smell of chewed cud,
Finished to a gleam by a ring in its nose.
Its dark slab is walled in by stones, a heavy, reserved glow.
A shot from the gun in the kitchen would tumble it to its knees,
Not surprised at its byre keeling over.

The gun is heavy and the child can just lift it
Teetering at arm's length to sight along the barrels.
Click. Click. The chambers of the gun's eyes are empty,
Their life a discharge of light into darkness
From red, waxed cartridges that plug into the breach
The stunning blond of their detonators.

The bull turns back the boulder of its head.

No one will harm it, it is a glass brimming with wine
That must be carried steadily to the guest.
The gun's isolation is taken onto the moor.
In a drizzle, spent cases are snapped from the breach
And left like symbols on the green edge of a path.

Parallel Lines

What a surprise:
The white surface
Of the moon, a face
In shock, hair torn off,

On what I thought
Was an ordinary
Day, floating in blue.
And here come gulls

In a keen cruise,
Intent on their doings
Like the motion
Of silence.

Blood and bone
Keep me trudging
While the gulls spill air
To harbour in a field

And the moon
Fades as if the future

Were a self-effacement
Into the past.

I Can't Keep Them Both

—"I can't keep them both, Ma. There's no money and he's always drunk."
At the bottom of the long cottage garden was a buttercup field.
In summer it was glazed with foot-high flowers.
—"Let's see if you like butter."
And Grandma leaned over the low wall to pick a spray,
Holding it to my chin.—"You do."
When the pig had to be killed, she fed it special scraps,
Rubbing its back with a broom.
But when the butcher came, with men to hold it down, she was stern.
I knelt by the bucket with a wooden spoon.
—"Stir it thoroughly."
The slash across the throat was quick and well-done,
And as it bucked and screamed, blood pumped into the bucket.
Then the pig relaxed, as if it had taken it kindly.
The men let go and it flopped to one side.
—"There you are, Mrs Fletcher."—"Thank you, Mr Jones."
I walked up to the end of the garden and stood at the wall.
Buttercups moved a shimmering cloth in the breeze.
—"Melva! Melva! Mecky!"
That year Grandma had held me up to a hedge where thrushes crammed a
    nest with their beaks;
But boys next door had stuffed them to the jaws with sand and they died.
Mother had been urgent in that talk in the kitchen.
The coconut matting had prickled my knees, linoleum cool on my palms,
As I listened, pressed close to the dark side of the door.

Out of the Fight

The black graves of the Cymry
On impossible slopes,
Giving back no light but
Absorbing all into the stone,

The colour of umbrellas
And sombre clothes and hushed
Conversation; future plans
Brought to an end

With the chisel's clean
Strokes. At dawn, even,
The lanes and roads are filled
By the whine of traffic,

A great army revving up,
Full of expectation,
About to launch an offensive
In all directions.

The absence of sound
About the stones cannot be
Broken; absolute zero
Of such active expectations.

Phantoms

Unstable as herds,
Ears pricked, heads turned
From their feeding. Men
Duck under wings
With fuel pipes; trucks

Sidle up with missiles.
The canopies bulge
As the eye that sees fear
In all directions.
It will stampede them,

Gazelles on the runway
Shimmering in giddy heat,
Lifting and folding their
Legs in an act of grace
As they leap with our lives.

The Town Where I Was Born

The town where I was born is surrounded by hills.
When the evening sky shone turquoise in summer, with small ribs of cloud,
And Venus wobbling its brilliance on the horizon,
The hills became solid black without any depth.
Even a farm light gave no perspective, or the lamps of a car
Bumping up to a flash then disappearing
As it twisted down a lane between banks and trees.
And when the night was grey with cloud from the Llangattock Mountains

To the Black Mountain across the Usk,

The hills were muggy and insecure, withdrawn without feature,

Except over the Blorenge where the under-surface of cloud had a reddish
    tinge

From the flaring of blast-furnaces in the town beyond.

There was a steady glow, with occasional flickering, like a colour of silence,

And I had to strain to think of the roar and shouts

As liquid steel trundled overhead in cauldrons on chains

To be poured with a shower of sparks in moulds

By men who moved quickly in the heat and glare.

Now things are different: I am another man and look at other hills.

Last night I stood on the doorstep after dark and stared into the east as if it
    were the past.

I could guess where Craig-y-Pistyll plunged down

As where was Bryn Garw among the invisible folds,

But all was embedded in dark. I thought: it is without and within,

Watching a car on the long track from Banc-y-Darren

Travel down through Cefn Llwyd, faltering lights that rose to a glare,

As if they were looking for something.

This time the cloud glowed too, and because the wind had veered through
    the day from south to east,

I could smell them burning, Birmingham and Coventry,

And the red glowering of the sky was the reflection of their flames,

And across Pumlumon, Liverpool and Manchester, and across Mynydd
    Epynt,

Cardiff and Bristol. The cloud slid steadily above me

And on the wind there was the smell of the fine dust of bricks

And the black dust of charcoal, and the grey dust of stones.

I never knew before how the smell of cities burning

Is like the must and acridity of old houses and the lives they have given up.

I remembered how in Cardiff after the war, we passed rows of façades

And nothing else standing, and how in a second-floor window for a year
There was a wine-glass intact, missed by the blast,
Placed there by the hand which had drained it and moved away
With a shining clarity, a salute and goodbye.

At Craig-y-Pistyll

At Craig-y-Pistyll there's a deserted house
This side of the rocky gully that takes excess water from the dam.
With the door ajar and burst from its hinges
I didn't need to knock before I went in,
And black-and-red tiles in square patterns
Led me to the living-room where grey light from a small window
Showed me tools with smooth handles no one had a use for,
And a long-shafted spade for pulling bread deftly from the oven
In a deep recess by the grate. And there were chairs, unvarnished,
And looking as though they were made to be patient in.
In the kitchen nothing but bare stone, and bottles on a shelf,
Green and brown glass with dust round the necks.
Going up the dried wood of the narrow stairs
Was still like intruding on privacy,
Bending to peer through dirty panes in low windows,
Wandering the four rooms across echoing planks.
But there were holes in the roof where slates had slipped
And the open sky was a greater intrusion.
In the shed outside there had been sheets of hardboard,
Beams of rough-cut wood (none of it new),
The hardboard buckling slightly from being stacked
At too broad an angle against the wall.
And wandering into a final bedroom
I found a double-bed wrapped in black polythene.

Lying back, I stared through a hole in the roof

And listened to wind in nearby trees.

Whoever had been here with timber and hardboard

Had lain as well on the damp-free shining mattress and slept,

Or not slept but turned at last on his back to look at the clouds flushed by

the moon

And clusters of stars that could have been galaxies

Shimmering faintly in the holes above his head.

Then he heard the silence as defined by leaves

And the intricate movements of a stream meandering in shallows a hundred

yards from the house.

The bread spade, the useless tools and the stripped farmhouse chairs had

been his,

Not the left-overs of people giving up and leaving the door open without

looking back

Following the bitter jutting of their jaws.

Even in summer he felt chilly on the bed

And at dawn got up for breakfast, too much like camping,

Then went to the shed and set-to at his work.

Whenever he stopped, the hush of trees entered him.

He listened, started again, leaned to the wood as the saw bit through his

pencil line.

A man can be absorbed by a place until he lives its life, wears its face

Looks out the door warily, with its eyes.

That last night he lay on the black bed and knew this,

Got up next day and walked down the track past the one workable farm,

Over the stepping stones of the stream,

Up the path that cuts across a spur of the hill,

Then along the grass lane until he came to Salem, where

As the tarmac passed hurriedly under the shadow of his feet

He took himself again to be the person that he was.

▪ INTERVIEW WITH JOHN BARNIE ▪

DL: As editor of *Planet, the Welsh Internationalist*, what criteria do you use in selecting articles, poetry, and fiction for publication?

JB: Most articles in *Planet* are commissioned. We go out looking for writers in areas we specifically want to cover. But for fiction and poetry we depend more on what comes in, though there are writers we do ask for work. I think in the end the criteria depend on editorial opinion. It is possible to say that you are open to all kinds of literature—but I know that's not true for myself. I think those who do say that are either deceiving themselves or deceiving their readers. I hope my tastes are broad, but there are limits. The danger is that something really good—the manuscript of "The Waste Land"—will reach your hands and you put it back in the envelope. You don't know if you're doing that.

DL: I suppose your editorial biases would mean that some writers simply won't send to *Planet*?

JB: I think there are writers who don't come to us. I suspect that some people perceive *Planet* as "academic" and "intellectual," using those terms in their modern debased form—"academic" can be a dirty word. My own view is that *Planet* is a popularizing magazine in a certain way. Thirty years ago there were several magazines like this in England, for example—magazines that assumed there would be a general reader who had interests across a range of disciplines, a general curiosity about life, about culture, about sociology, history, science, as well as poetry and short stories. That's the tradition that *Planet* derives from, and it's the tradition we want to maintain. I think educational development in the '70s, which seemed to broaden the potential for higher education for a larger number of people, also narrowed it because of the political ethos in which that education occurred. As I said, "academic" these days can be used to put down writing which attempts to approach questions of the mind or broach broad issues in society or culture at a reasonably complex level.

DL: Are there criteria by which you select those writers you commission?

JB: Compared to the other Anglo-Welsh magazines, *Planet* has a broader base of interest—sociology, the environment, politics, and so on. So we're often looking for a different kind of writer. For example, we recently ran a series of articles on science and society by Phil Williams, who is professor of astronomy at the university in Aberystwyth. If it's a subject we think we ought to cover, we try to find the best person in that particular field to write the article. We'd be looking for someone with a high level of expertise, who can also write in a clear, jargon-free style.

DL: Would it be fair to say that the English-language poetry and fiction you are interested in demonstrates some kind of a Welsh identity, a particular cultural stance?

JB: Not in any simple or obvious way, partly because I'm not sure what a Welsh identity means any more. I feel that whereas there was a very strong Anglo-Welsh identity in writers of the '30s, '40s, and '50s—up through the generation which includes Meic Stephens and Tony Conran and so on—in the generation of writers that has come to prominence in the last twenty years, there is less of a sense of being Welsh or Anglo-Welsh (though many of them would probably deny this). I feel increasingly that there is a slide, an inevitable cultural pressure towards Anglicization in Wales, though for obvious reasons this is a very contentious issue.

Welsh identity depends on some kind of relationship to the Welsh language. The idea that there can be a sort of autonomous, English-language culture in Wales has some academic support and is axiomatic for a number of contemporary Anglo-Welsh poets and short story writers. But that idea seems to be less and less verifiable in terms of the literature being produced. Increasingly, poetry and stories coming out of English-speaking Wales are really not distinguishable from the literature coming out of England. There really is a sense in which writers of the '30s and '40s—some of them at least, such as Gwyn Jones, Glyn Jones, or the Thomases—were using English in ways that are different from English writers and which can be seen as the beginnings of a quite distinctive literary tradition. But if you look at the background of most of those people, they themselves were Welsh-speakers or had a residual Welsh-speaking background, through their parents. I think the socioeconomic developments of the '60s, '70s and '80s seriously eroded if not eradicated that tradition or potential tradition.

DL: Do you receive submissions cast in a self-consciously Anglo-Welsh style? In theory, certain signs of Welshness in part define Anglo-Welsh poetry. Some of those might be authentic and earned, but others might be forced, designed to help a poem fit into "the Anglo-Welsh tradition" and thus improve its chances for publication.

JB: You get some of that, but not as much as I would have expected, and over the eight years I've been at *Planet* I've seen less and less. What you get is more and more poetry which is undistinguishable from English poetry. It's wrong to say it's not distinguishable from "Anglo-American" poetry because American poetry strikes me as being basically very different from English. There's almost a language barrier between American and English or British poetry. So the answer is we don't get much of what you describe.

There are a number of poets doing interesting work—I particularly like the recent poems of Christine Evans, for example. And then there's Mike Jenkins who in the past few years has been experimenting with a kind of dialect poetry which we've been publishing in *Planet*. He works with something like a transcription of the working-class speech of Merthyr Tudful (where he teaches) and other Valleys industrial towns and villages. I think what he is producing is quite innovative and exciting. "Transcription" perhaps isn't quite the right word to describe what he does—the language of the poems is more a literary equivalent, an illusion of speech, which draws on the inventiveness of Valleys' idiom but intensifies it.

DL: *Planet* has commissioned long poems by Gillian Clarke and Jean Earle. And in a recent issue of *Planet* there's a long poem by R. S. Thomas. Have you been deliberately encouraging larger poetic projects?

JB: We commissioned six poets to write long poems because I was under the impression that the long poem was virtually dead. We did that in 1985, and since then we've been inundated with long poems, or poem sequences. I had no idea that so many people were writing them. The long poem isn't dead; it just isn't getting published. And there are good reasons why not, judging from some submissions. In retrospect it was an experiment about which I now have reservations. The idea of the long poem is exciting but it is an extremely difficult form to succeed in. We were probing to see if we could pull some people out. We did publish one or two good poems in that series of commissions.

In America the long poem is more common. *American Poetry Review*, for example, publishes poems of some length frequently. They're not necessarily better or more successful, but in America I think there's a sense that the long poem is a viable form. In Wales at least—or in English-speaking Wales—there is not so strong a feeling that it can be done. There's a greater concentration on the lyric, which goes back to your initial point. I do have a prejudice against the overtly autobiographical lyric. Not that I think it can't be successful—I'm a great admirer of Robert Lowell and Sylvia Plath. But that kind of deeply personal poetry has its limits. It can descend into a sort of snapshot poetry—handing round your family album. Much poetry of this sort is the result of a failure to realize that intense personal or family experience has to be *recreated* as a kind of fiction. It's a failure to realize that poetry *is* fiction.

DL: Robert Lowell, though, wrote personal lyrics which incorporate social and political dimensions.

JB: *History* is one of his greatest books. I think it's significant that people focus on *Life Studies* and to a lesser extent *For the Union Dead* as his classic books and tend to dismiss or ignore *Notebooks* and *History*. But the latter are precisely where Lowell broadens out and brilliantly maintains that balance between intense personal poems and very public poetry. There's always this sense of the *projection* of a person—"Robert Lowell," like "R. S. Thomas," is not the man you see in the street, carrying a shopping bag. He's a literary production, a fiction, and the people who send in the stuff that we keep sending back don't perceive that need to create a fiction.

DL: Can you comment about your perception of the difference between the original *Planet* and the *Planet* you are now helping to edit?[1]

JB: The magazine was, then, a campaigning magazine with a program of fairly left-wing politics within a Welsh nationalist framework. To that extent it reflected and helped forge a certain line of thinking within the Welsh intelligentsia which came to a head in the 1979 referendum. It's not entirely coincidental that Ned Thomas closed the magazine down in the same year.

The situation in Wales in the '90s is very different, its politics in some ways more diffuse and lacking in any clear direction. *Planet* has maintained a clear line on such issues as the Welsh language and the need for greater autonomy from England, but it's also far more fully committed to environmental issues which were barely on the horizon in the late '70s but which now can't be ignored.

DL: Interest in language politics seems to distinguish the current generation of Anglo-Welsh poets from the older generation—the younger poets are not so interested in the language issue.

JB: It depends. Greg Hill is certainly very involved in language, and Christopher Meredith as well as other younger writers. But I think it is true that the younger generation do not by and large have the same sense that Welsh identity is inextricably bound up with some sort of relationship to the Welsh language. Seren Books has done a very good job of creating a poetry press in Wales under extremely difficult circumstances. Cary Archard said at the launch for the *Poetry Wales* Green Issue, quite rightly, that Seren Books has become one of the half-dozen best poetry presses in Britain. Getting good reviews in metropolitan journals such as the *Times Literary Supplement* is a sign that it's gaining a wider British reputation. But the cost of that recognition—or perhaps one of the reasons for it—is that most Seren poets would fit quite easily in a metropolitan London-oriented context. This is not a question of whether they are good poets or bad poets. Although Seren is in its way a very good press, it is a press which reflects that slow slide into Anglicization.

DL: Because you've resettled in Wales, are publishing poetry in Wales, and are learning Welsh, many would call you an Anglo-Welsh poet. Since you argue that most Anglo-Welsh poetry is really provincial English poetry, would you be content to describe yourself as a provincial English poet?[2]

JB: No, I wouldn't be *content*. But I think that's probably true. I don't see what I've written up to now, or what I've published up to now, as Welsh in any way. I've never claimed to be an Anglo-Welsh poet, or any kind of poet. I would say that what I write derives from the border area where I come from. I was Anglicized from the beginning.

DL: Should R. S. Thomas call himself a Welsh writer?

JB: He's taken an extreme position, which is that the only Welsh writers are those who write in Welsh. I've a lot of sympathy with that position. Bobi Jones, who was born an English speaker, is a Welsh writer by virtue of the fact that he writes in Welsh.[3] But I would say that R. S. Thomas *is* a Welsh writer—and this is where it gets tricky and unprovable—by virtue of the fact that he has aligned himself so clearly with the Welsh language. He's close to being bilingual and writes prose in Welsh. In my opinion he is an archetypal Welsh writer in English.

Dylan Thomas, who is widely seen as the archetypal Welsh writer in English, especially abroad, is really the obverse. He was in his way a brilliant but fatally flawed writer. He never grew up, never became an adult. His best poems are about his inability to transform himself into a grownup, and his great stories and *Under Milk Wood*—terrific, comic stuff in its way—created an image of Wales which has been fatal to Welsh identity in England and America in that it has portrayed Wales as a comic place full of marvelous, avuncular characters, quaint sayings, quaint uses of English, but comic and not, in the end, what you take seriously. Saunders Lewis burns down a bombing school, goes to jail, loses his job—you have to take a man like that seriously.[4] He's a Welsh extremist. Dylan Thomas isn't a Welsh extremist, he's a Welsh performer, a stage personality, and he's pushed a stage version of Wales to its limits in a way which still reverberates catastrophically. R. S. is Dylan Thomas's contemporary; in fact he's a year older. He doesn't have the same international reputation, yet in my opinion he's a far greater poet. What I'm saying now is partly a reaction against an early sense that Dylan was *the* Welsh poet—Dylan Thomas was Wales to me when I was sixteen and seventeen.

Going back to your other question—it was through reading the *Planet* of the '70s, through trying to learn Welsh, through reading people like R. S.

and Saunders Lewis, that I realized to what extent Dylan Thomas is a parody of Wales.

DL: In American anthologies of modern poetry, you don't see much representation of R. S. Thomas.

JB: If I'm right that R. S. Thomas actually has achieved that sense of Welsh identity through the medium of English, I think one reason why he doesn't have easy access to an international audience is that he is so very Welsh. There's an extremist, puritan, honed-down Biblical edge to what he writes, and it's not so easily open to access as the poetry of Dylan Thomas. If you came from Dylan's south Wales—and I was brought up on the edge of it— all that Dylan Thomas stuff about sex and death, and so on, was part of growing up in a world where sex was a taboo subject. It seemed daring to refer to it obliquely, and often obscurely, in modernistic or symbolist imagery. But it's really the worst kind of provincialism masquerading as international modernism. His best poetry opens out into a much clearer and, in a true sense, pathetic vision, a statement about somebody who is powerless to be born into full adulthood, full consciousness.

DL: Will Anglo-Welsh poetry become established, or will it fade completely into English provincial literature?

JB: I think that the battle may well be over. There is now an established Anglo-Welsh literature with a press and magazines, and inclusion in that literature is defined by the fact that you write about Wales or you come from Wales. So writers coming to Wales become Anglo-Welsh poets by virtue of living in Wales. What happens to them when they move back to England? Are they suddenly not Anglo-Welsh poets? There is in a sense an official Anglo-Welsh literary culture which I feel is increasingly false, based upon the premise that since there's been a tradition established, coming out of the 1920s and '30s, it must be permanently viable. It doesn't take into account the fact that the political, economic, and linguistic relationship with England is constantly changing. Despite all the efforts of Cymdeithas yr Iaith,[5] all the, if you like, extremist responses of the '60s and '70s, the Anglo-Welsh world is constantly moving towards increased Anglicization. So you have this unreal situation, an apparently established Anglo-Welsh literature which looks increasingly like the king with no clothes.

DL: In the Welsh Arts Council grant-giving system, some editors and publishers get block grants and some have to apply for grants for specific books. Some people think this system has been effective in promoting writing in Wales, while others argue that it's promoting a conservative writing environment, inhibiting experimentation. If you've got a grant to fall back on, won't you be less likely to go out and create the audience you need for a certain book, or the audience for a magazine? Don't the monies that support the publication of poetry determine the content of what's published?

JB: Everybody I talk to in the literary world who gets a grant dismisses the idea that because you are grant aided you are unaware of, or cavalier about, the need for a market and the need to promote and keep high standards. I agree. The fact that you do get public money, in *Planet*'s case a substantial grant, makes you intensely aware of the need to do the best you can, to create the best magazine which it is within your power to create. I think the fact that book sales and magazine sales in Wales look low in relation to a purely commercial concern is based on the assumption that a large sector of the population of three million is potentially going to read at a fairly high level. But the readership for a magazine like *Planet* or a poetry magazine like *Poetry Wales* or for poetry books is, in the present cultural climate, inevitably small. In a small country like Wales, a nation like Wales, you simply can't sustain a literary culture at present without public money. If you are an English conservative, you'd say, too bad—the market rules and any such pretensions to culture must go under. So far in Wales that view has not prevailed. The Welsh Arts Council grants maintain a strong and basically fair balance between the Welsh and Anglo-Welsh cultures. I think that literary culture is by and large not sustainable in Wales without grants. That is partly a product of the small size of the readership. But a nation like Denmark, for instance, would consider it quite right and automatic that literary culture be supported by the state.

DL: Your poem sequence, *Clay*, focuses on the lives of English romantic poets. Where did your interest in that subject come from?

JB: When we came back to south Wales from Denmark in 1982, we lived hand to mouth, and I took on a variety of jobs. One was teaching for the Open University in Cardiff. I got the chance to teach a course on the romantics. Having never taught the romantics, I had to read them very intensively for about a year. I found myself being drawn consistently from the academic criticism, which I found tedious, to biographies. So the poems came out of that very intense reading of the biographies. In retrospect, I think one reason they appealed to me is that unresolvable tension between art and life. Most of them screwed up their lives completely and at the same time wrote some of the finest poetry in English—that made a great impression on me.

DL: The poems are written in a personal voice but use a persona, fictionalizing real literary characters' voices. Aren't you writing a kind of modern confessional poem?

JB: I wasn't aware of any such intention when I was writing the sequence, but I think now that you're probably right.

DL: I suspected the poems had to come out of teaching, where you become so absorbed by the subject matter.

JB: Yes, but I've taught many other writers and have been absorbed by them. I greatly admire the modernists, for instance, but I've not written about T. S. Eliot or Ezra Pound in sequences, and those poets have had a bigger influence on me than the romantics.

DL: Your collection of essays *The King of Ashes* contains chapters focusing on various subjects. But one of the unifying threads concerns identity, a postmodern identity.

JB: I have for years hated the term "postmodern," and I've recently come to realize that's because I'm a product of it. I thought when I grew up in Abergavenny, a close-knit community—and I came from a lower middle-class shopkeeper background—that I belonged to a stable world which would never change. Then I went to university and became educated in English literature, went abroad, and began to try to put some of these things together.

I came to realize that they can't be put together, that the modern experience, at least for me, has been one of discord, of the breaking down of assurances regarding what you are and where you come from. So the book is really about how any perception you may have these days of some kind of integration is a chance pattern of cultural/personal interest. I say "chance," but in a way it's historically determined. It's governed by chance in that you are potentially open to a huge array of cultural influences which only *seem* like choice. Blues and Texas-Mexican music—those are among my "choices," but they come out of a cultural situation where choice is meaningless, where the huge array of choice actually destroys meaning.

DL: Since publishing *The King of Ashes* in 1989 you've written a book of poetry and fiction, *The Confirmation*, a fictional work, *The City*, as well as *Y Felan a Finnau*, a study of the blues, published in Welsh. Can you comment on why these last few years have been so productive for you?

JB: I'd known for a long time that I wanted to write an extended piece about my early experience in the border town of Abergavenny in the 1940s and '50s, but I could never find a suitable form. Then, a few years ago, I read the autobiographical novels of the Swedish poet Harry Martinson, *Nässlorna blomma* (*The Nettles are Flowering*) and *Vägen ut* (*The Way Out*), and they gave me a form which I knew I could use—short, discontinuous sections (hardly chapters) in which Martinson projected his childhood freely as a symbolic fiction. I wrote the prose section of *The Confirmation* very quickly in the summer of 1989.

Equally, I wanted to write for some time about my experience of city life—I've lived for twenty years or so in cities like Birmingham, Nottingham, and Copenhagen—but again I was never able to hit on a suitable form. Then in 1990 during our annual visit to relatives in Copenhagen, it struck me that I could use Martinson's form to write about what was, to me, the disjunctive and alienating experience of city life. When we came back I wrote *The City*, again very quickly.

Y Felan a Finnau was a commission. I had a year in which to write it; so I knuckled down and did that, and not much else, in 1991.

The Common Land

1.

Streams are boundaries of the common land,
the air above them scored with mosquitoes
in a single-pitched treble,
lines of flight-paths for swallows
swinging down from telephone high-wires.

Alive with spring, geese once came down
to dip their poker beaks
and shake off fleas and ticks
wings oaring water, stretching
necks towards a rare sun.

Sometimes streams send messengers
like the dragonfly, coptering alone

with waxen wings on the verge of melting
to leave the seam of its body
and anthracite eyes embedded in the sill.

2.

Conifers form a strata of heavy green
between rough pasture and horizon:
the width of a motorway from here,
jagged outline blurred by distance.

Hump-backed hillocks bleat,
surfaces amenable as womb-walls
to springing lambs, whose white
is the hard winter turned wool.

A flat track maps the old tram-line:
a child with skin cut to rags
by blades of dark, a woman whose phlegm
was solid as lumps she'd cut.

No way into these drift-mines now:
sand-coloured grass has crept
progressively over slag, still
there are black grazes where soil can't scab.

3.

Burning up the danger sign
in a blast of exhaust, the young man
rope-kidnaps the reclaimed heaps
with his scrambling-track.

Shorn sheep are sent startled
by his acceleration, he's the hub
of the scene now, his noise in spokes
reaches further than fence or forest.

4.

Weekends and the sun transform the land
to a park. Past cows' whipping tails
and twitching ears, go the couples
disappearing into a gully of shade.

When they return, coiled like ivy,
they bob past the bog-cotton heads,
four-legged beasts observed curiously
by young girls flicking mane-long hair;

under branches of watchmen oaks
they've put up tents, sitting bored outside
they pull out tufts and wait
to see what catch the sun will bring.

5.

When storms come the sky
tries to uproot the whole hillside,
rain has sharp claws and clumps
of reeds bow in submission.

The horses had sensed this coming,
flinging a breeze from haunches,
rumbling as they stamped hooves,
cutting the air into ditches.

Clouds plummet where they circled:
a crow's drowning in the wind,
branches thrash, trunks tread water.
A leaf's taken in its green prime:

it's lost as borders are bursting.
The only light left on the common land
are the disc-shaped marshy pools
growing where horses printed their sound.

Chartist Meeting

Heolgerrig, 1842

The people came to listen
looking down valley as they tramped;
the iron track was a ladder
from a loft to the open sea—
salt filling the air like pollen.

Each wheel was held fast
as you would grip a coin;
yet everything went away from them.
The black kernel of the mountains
seemed endless, but still in their stomachs
a furnace-fire roared,
and their children's eyes hammered
and turned and hollowed out a cannon.

Steam was like a spiral of wool
threaded straight down the valley,

lost past a colliery.
The tramways held the slope
as though they were wood of a pen.
Wives and children were miniatures
of the hill, the coal engrained
in enclosures on their skin.

They shook hands with the sky,
an old friend; there, at the field,
oak trees turned to crosses
their trunks bent with the weight
of cloud and wind, and harsh grass
from marshes that Morgan Williams,
the weaver, could raise into a pulpit.

Invisible Times

Living in invisible times:
loneliness an economist's art.

Into the phone I take care:
testing the colour of each word
because of the spy whose wire
antennaes twitch, whose mouth
is a metal tube my voice falls down
to be shred like paper.

Outside, I wear a crustaceous coat,
knowing that the rain avenges
those gun-barrel chimneys

who wage war on the sky.
One day my scales will be eaten away
and flesh frazzled to cinders.

All around are the sick people
who cannot find the germs.
I tell them where to look:
under switches which grow on fingertips,
in clocks whose hands are trees
and pylons and flags.

Every day I'm on this journey:
looking for the computer who told
those lies, who caused my rejection.
"Facts are seeds grown hard
as bullets," I would inform it.
But my search is aimless,
because the computer whirrs
in too many skulls to crack open.

The expert tells me I'm mad.
I see the motorway that workmen
are laying behind his grin:
it runs from the city of emotion
to the city of reason
and all purpose is within its rims.

The Beach, my Son and the alltime Batman

We drape ourselves down
we are the same
as those posing we condemn
soaking up sunlight
not innocently but complacently
reading about it
as chemicals magnify the rays
we drive along we buy
the things that cannot burn.

My son has made his nest
in front of me I tell him
of the north and ice melting
the next flood the cities
are a ball the oceans
a bat above them
the hole above us widens
we will fall upwards
into the gap and together
drift into space.

The cities drown as the tide
hurries in and people quickly
busy their belongings he sees
the need to swim
but how can we learn
to swim in space?
there is no air the tanks
will surely drag us down.

That night he dreams catastrophe
the trees have lost their skin
they all drop to the ground
and roots break up
into pieces of a desert
but God the alltime Batman
comes to the rescue when
my son lifted to a cloud
rides to the sun
makes peace between
Water and Fire at last
so everything grows a beginning.

Returning to the Nant

i

The tarmac-glistening road
ahead of us, the end
of the world the king Gwrtheyrn
sought, but our own sojourn.
Village below, down sheer
cliffs . . . our nerves braking.
A Peregrine Falcon swoops.

ii

Strike a match, make our lightning.
In our fire is his castle
split like an oak: proud
as it was, overlooking the coast.
We position wood, contain the flames.

Our children paddle in the sea
throwing pebbles, naming them
(as Gwrtheyrn had the stars)
unaware of the danger:
cancer in the unsuspecting crab.

iii

A single yellow poppy:
the moon fallen to beach.
Goats are the kings of the Nant
watching from the disused quarry
as we struggle, hobble and complain
up paths of moving stones.
They stand still, for a moment
growing out of rock like the flower.
Till the one, larger, balances on ledges
and screes, shifting the mountain down.

iv

Acres of granite chippings,
yet the three abandoned quarries
look like a Zorba's folly.
Once core for Liverpool's roads:
making easier the tread of slavemaster,
black boots of whipping leather
the colour and shine of tarmacadam
which pushed granite aside;
amenable then stubborn successor.

Llithfaen: a place of granite.
But 'Ar Werth' signs
are flags of mourning.

In the Nant, workers' terraces
linked arm-to-arm, with rooms
the size of the manager's hearth;
his garden-walls steep
as the face they'd worked.

In seaside towns, shopkeepers recognize
no price for Cymraeg
as English trippers buy mugs
with dragon prints from assistants
whose Saesneg is deliberate phrases
punctuated by the checkout's calculating.

vi

Circled around the teacher:
a torc close to the throat.
An 'O' as a butty was called
in the echo of a mining gallery.

We're gathering expressions
like beachcombers after rare colours:
displaying them for approval, children again.

For each one the 'O' becomes
something special they're retrieving:
hoop of schoolyard, a lost ring,

or the face of a grandfather
speaking a language he later disowned.

Gurnos Boy

I come from-a ewgest 'state in town,
second ewgest maze in Ewrop, they say,
coz planners potched it up, the clowns:
I'd give em a proper lampin
on'y they've all gone away.

Life gets so bloody borin
I'd sooner read-a graffiti
than stay in-a ouse snorin:
latest is MAGIC MUSH, writin like spaghetti
thrown over walls, adverts f' sin.

Ower streets wuz named afta trees
t' make em sound natural, innit?
But yew mostly ave Nature b'yer
when yew tread in-a shit,
or see dogs umpin in threes!

At-a school on top o' the ill
where I ewsed t' bunk if I ad-a chance,
we wore uniform fit fer a funeral,
the on'y way yew could advance
wuz if yew give em no jip, wern a rebel.

The state o' ower ome is beyond:

we got ot an cold runnin water
down-a walls an windows an a pond
in-a livin-room, which we oughta
convert into a tidy sauna!

This place is gettin famous f' murderers,
we produce em like Oovers washing-machines.
If this Government push me much further
I'll afta cut them posh people clean
in theyr big ouses with burglar larms.

Carn wait f' Monday t' come round:
Giro cheque droppin like a gulp o' beer
an lastin just as long. The sound
o' money like-a rain tampin down
afta drought on ower cracked reservoirs.

Among the Debris

Ee were a brill teacher, ee were.
Ewsed t' tell us stories
playin cards underwater
is leg trapped in a giant clam.

But every so often
ee'd go mental, throw a wobbly,
grabbin ower desks an chairs
as we woz scribblin appily
an fling em flyin
is eyes explodin like gas,

is screams pick-axin
into ower yer-drums,
ower mouths woz gulpin,
we wuz so stunned!

An afta, ee always passed
a bagful o' sorries round,
tellin us ow ee still
could yer that sound:
a slow, unnatural thunder
of movin ground an ow
ee wuz searchin fer them lost children,
buryin is ands in slurry
till ee found us, sittin
among the debris.

· ROBERT MINHINNICK ·

The Drinking Art

   The altar of glasses behind the bar
Diminishes our talk. As if in church
The solitary men who come here
Slide to the edges of each black
Polished bench and stare at their hands.
   The landlord keeps his own counsel.

   This window shows a rose and anchor
Like a sailor's tattoo embellished
In stained glass, allows only the vaguest
Illumination of floor and ceiling,
The tawny froth the pumps sometimes spew.
   And the silence settles. The silence settles

Like the yellow pinpoints of yeast
Falling through my beer, the bitter
That has built the redbrick
Into the faces of these few customers,
Lonely practitioners of the drinking art.
　　Ashtrays, a slop-bucket, the fetid

　　Shed-urinal, all this I wondered at,
Running errands to the back-doors of pubs,
Woodbines and empty bottles in my hands.
Never become a drinking-man, my
Grandmother warned, remembering Merthyr
　　And the Spanish foundrymen

　　Puking their guts up in the dirt streets,
The Irish running from the furnaces
To crowd their paymaster into a tavern,
Leather bags of sovereigns bouncing on his thigh.
But it is calmer here, more subtly dangerous.
　　This afternoon is a suspension of life

　　I learn to enjoy. But now
The towel goes over the taps and I feel
The dregs in my throat. A truce has ended
And the clocks start again. Sunlight
Leaps out of the street. In his shrine of glass
　　The landlord is wringing our lives dry.

The Looters

The helicopter cameras
Bring us the freeze frames.
A black sea outlines each peninsula
As snow finer than marble dust
Blurs the steeples of the spruce.
Bad weather, the wisdom goes,
Brings a community together.
Tonight the screen is a mirror
And the news is us.

At a house in Bedlinog
A drift has left its stain
Like a river in flood
Against the highest eaves.
There will be a plaque placed there soon
As if for some famous son,
While the cataract at Cwm Nash
Is a thirty foot long stalactite
Full of eyes and mouths
And the dazzling short circuits
Of a pillar of mercury.
An icicle uncirclable by three men.

Abandoned on the motorway
The container lorries are dislocated
Vertebrae. The freeze has broken
The back of our commerce
While on the farms, the snow-sieged
Estates, people return
To old technologies.

Meat is hung in double rows,
The carcasses identified
By the slashing beams.
Each one looms hugely,
Puzzling as a chrysalis
Under its silver condom of frost.
They sway like garments on a rack
When padlocks break and the freezer-
Doors swing out. It is too cold
Here to trail blood, where bread
Is frozen into breeze-blocks
And ten thousand tubes of lager
Sparkle under their ripping caul.
As flashlights zigzag up the wall
Tights turn red and tropical bronze
In each thin wallet.

The stranded drivers sleep in schools,
Their groups determined to uphold
The constitution of the snow.
Families smile through thermos-steam,
A child with her kitten, blue
As a cinder, sucking a blanket:
The usual cast of winter's news
As the commentary runs its snowplough
Through the annihilating white.

Outside, the cars are scoops
Of cumulus, and toboggans
Polish gutters in the drifts.
We never see the looters.

They move somewhere in the darkness
Through the blizzard, beyond the thin
Bright crescent of the screen,
Those people who have understood the weather
And make tomorrow's news.

Development Area

The chimneys work all shifts,
Flying their pennants of flame.
And where technicians crash
A ball about, the corals
Are a jumbled alphabet
In the tar.

At Crymlyn the prehistoric
Debris works out of the soil
Its monument to amnesia:
Plastics and metal and fine
Blue polythene
Like the wrappings of a city.

It's a territory of sirens;
But step behind the lorry park
And sulphur falls with the dew,
While down on the glossy bark
Of the birches runs lichen
Like a lipsticked kiss.

Offices are hourglasses,
Secretaries their grains of sand.
On the glacier of the city's
Rubbish the children pick
For futures already discarded.
There is light here, but no window.

'What's the Point of Being Timid When the House Is Falling Down?'

Rumour, like blood, must circulate.
In movement it renews itself.

It was bleak, you said.
Wales was on the dole, and nobody cared;

The poets were in the traps
Waiting for the hare to come back;

In the country of the apathetic
The half-hearted man is king.

The fescue bleached, and the spiked bobbins of the teazle
Tip back and forth to the wind's pulse.

You had just made out
A staggering travel-expenses claim:

Train and bus I know give no free rides,
But John, I was driving you home.

For some reason I am digging,
Bruising my heel on the spade's blue shoulder.

And, creature of the great indoors,
It was strange that I should see you last

Walking up the Merthyr Road,
That ravaged sheepskin an affront to Whitchurch decency.

Six inches down I unearth a seam of frost,
Pale as anteggs, running into the dark.

Four in the morning is no time
To rediscover a savage malt:

The barman in pyjamas stared in weary disbelief;
Then turned, found the optics, and pressed.

It's all around me I suppose,
The invisible life of late winter

Accelerating now, an unstoppable rumour.
About you, famous drinkers,

Earnest lyric souls, and the merely loud
Had turned to wax.

There's something here that's at its end,
And something already edging into its place.

Make it a double, you grinned,
Savouring reunion with the Gaelic smoke.

The magpies in the hawthorn repair their dome,
In the barrels ice shrinks to a small dark embryo.

After all, a Sunday in Llandrindod
Offers no mercy to the squeamish.

The Mansion

The house stands as it always has,
Its windows tall above the lake
And grass cut almost to the yellow root.

Along the drive a whitelimed kerb
Follows a perfect crescent,
As if stone, like air or water, moved in waves.

My steps dissolve in gardens where
The acid rhododendron thrives,
Its flowers pink and white as naked dolls.

It always was a selfish tree,
Devouring the light, growing
Glossy and alone, the strong inheritor.

At the door they take my card
And a name in silver italics
Grants entry where I never thought to pass.

These hands laid gently on my arm
Disturb an earlier trespasser,
That child under the yew hedge

Who watched the long cars slide through his village
And women shaped like candleflames
Moving over the lawns.

Above his head the berries swelled
As soft as wax around each nucleus,
The black nugget of poison that would grow.

The Stones Themselves

Our children choose the life outside,
Needling the eyes of a pomegranate,
Making dens behind the bramble-curtained graves.

Death and devotion mean nothing
To their play, these tablets that we fail
To read flaking like birch-bark,

Notched with a language
Blurred as the scars of ivy on the church.
The stones themselves must know exhaustion here

And lean together like old men
In some hateful conspiracy.
An old man's evening, stone-dusk, drifts within the room.

And I would soon leave but for her
Wedged into a corner of the floor
That crackles with religious dust,

This globe-woman, squat as a pomegranate,
A grinning thalidomide shape
Holding herself hugely apart.

She smiles from her belly through the church
Offering us the honeycomb
Which these shrunken men refused to sip.

Unhistoried and unexplained
No coin in the charity box saves her.
I listen for her children in the dark.

Looking for Arthur

Now here was a valley stranger than most
In the legends. A heap of rusted cars
Lay racked like toast, and the pool of green
Nitrogen simmered between rocks.

We expected distant shouts,
Some land-manager's pursuit of our trespassing,
But only the silence accosted us
As we moved under the wall of the engine-house,

Higher, it seemed, than a cathedral,
Its gorgeous brickwork prickly with red moss,

And left the known world behind.
The mountain wore a scarf of mist

And below us now the buzzard
Floated like a fallen handkerchief.
I climbed in silence, middle-aged respect,
But the children creased the solemn tarns

With handfulls of the scree, dragging
Wellies through those cauldrons in the peat.
They swung on ropes of voices to the crown,
To discover that we were explorers

Of what someone else already knew,
But to retrieve from the cave's maw
This one horseshoe, whose rusting leaves
As yew-wood does, a regal dust

Against the skin, and glimpse the ocean's
Pale eyelid winking in its notch,
While at our feet a hare lay pressed
As flat as ruined corn.

The haggard and the falconer

To make a hawk, he sits up and starves
with her; stays with her through the pangs,
the hooded blindness, the sleeplessness aching
in the bones: three days and nights. The effect,
oddly, is to bond them, as torturers
the world over could tell you. Afterwards
they're a team: she'll fly for him
and her own pleasure, wear his colours,
take food from his hand, save
her meat for him.

   There are some, though,
that will not, and until she flies,
he has no way of knowing. A haggard
is a hawk that takes no partner

and shares nothing. Her keen eyes watch
her own chance; the dizzy vertical stoop
from the air, that catches the throat,
is for her; the kill her profit
and her delight.

   So he sits,
light-headed, chilled with hunger,
watching her; awake wondering
what she is; whether he has her.
Some say a haggard is the fault
of the falconer; a want
of devotion; he mustn't fail her.
While she is making, he'll scarcely see
his wife: he went in briefly
two nights ago, before he started
the hawk. His wife, as usual,
lay unmoved, watching him
under her eyelids.

When he has gone, she gives
herself ecstacies, fetching, in the dark,
great raucous breaths, heart hammering,
bright-eyed, exhausted. She could show
him how, but she will not: her love life
needs no helpmate, and if you can fly,
why share it?

The Frozen Field

I saw a flat space
by a river: from the air
a jigsaw-piece. It is green
by times, and brown, and golden,
and white. When green, it gives food
to animals: when golden,
to men. Brown, it is ridged
and patterned, but when white,
a plane of evenness.

When frost touches it by night,
it turns silver: blue shadows
etch the hollows, grassblades glitter
in the grip of silence. It was
in such a place as this,
elsewhere, on the coldest night
of a cold winter, two boys
drove a car, with some difficulty,
over the frozen hummocks: parked
in the breathtaking chill, the stillness
that weighed each leaf down,
and shot each other.

It was a place I knew
years ago: I must have seen
the field, in summer maybe,
growing turnips, grazing cattle,
dotted with the white
of sheep, the blue and orange

of tents, and all the time
travelling toward one night
vast with misery; the sharp cracks,
one-two, like branches in frost,
that broke the silence.

Who knows what a field
has seen? Maldon sounds
of marsh birds, boats, the east wind.
The thin wail across the mudflats
is a heron or a gull, not Wulfmaer,
the boy who chose to die
with his king, never having guessed
how long dying could take.

And an oak lives
a long time, but a nail-hole
soon closes. Of all the oaks
at Clontarf, which is the one
where Ulf Hreda nailed one end
of a man's guts, and walked him
round and round the tree, unwinding
at every step?

The night the boys died,
their field was Maldon was Clontarf,
was Arbela, Sedgemoor, Solferino,
was every field where a moon
has risen on grass stiff
with blood, on silvered faces.
. . . Aughrim was so white,

they said, with young bones,
it would never need lime again:
better not to see
in the mind's eye Magenta,
that named a new dye.

It was as if the field
clenched all this in
on itself, hunched over
the pain of all young men
since time began; as if
every crop it ever bore
crowded in on it: barley, blood,
sheep, leisure, suicide,
sorrow, so much, its being
could not stay in bounds
but spilled out over space
and time, unwinding
meanings as it went.

They tangle around
the field's riddle now: *I saw a stage*
for pain, a suffering-space.
The fine mist of aloneness closed it
in the morning: at sunset
it was flooded with blood.

Thinking such things often,
we should see too much. I see
a picnic place, a playground.
My eyes half-open, I lean

against a tree; hear through the ground
children's feet chasing.
The sunlight shivers: *someone*
walked over my grave. I chew
on a stiff grassblade.

Frankincense

The sweet gums live
in silver, locked away
in my vestry, till it comes time
to fill the aisles, the cold
high spaces with them. Even
their names went to my head:
resin and frankincense.

No-one slept. The gunfire
started before dawn. I went
to my church; prayed for the boys
from our village, and for the firing
not to come any closer.

About mid-morning,
the King's men nearly kicked
the door in. They had carts
piled high with wounded: all
our people that weren't dead,
and they just left them.

We laid them on pews,
their skull wounds soaking
into hassocks: all the bright colours
drowned in one. Their moans echoed
in song's space, and each day
the reek of festered flesh
crept higher, further.

They took them away
after a week. Women set
to scrubbing stone and wood,
while I burned incense
into sweet, dense smoke.

Now again the clean
empty, old-stone smell
fills the walls. At Epiphany,
when I tell my flock the coming
of the Magi, my guts clench
on one word, the stench of suffering.

Railway signals

Welsh Industrial & Maritime Museum

This is a good place for those things to wait
whose use is over. It ends a wide street
going nowhere: artery of the failing trade
whose handsome derelict buildings were left stranded
by the ebb-tide; banks, exchanges,
chandlers, all quietly minding their lost business.

Inside the museum, the old machines
wear fresh paint. They still work; piston-engines
drive nothing round, running smooth as ever,
pulleys lift air, boilers supply power
to nowhere in particular. Outside,
a pilot cutter settles in the weed

within sight of the sea. The tide's out;
between the moorings, wooden piles jut
from the mud, each bearing a railway signal.
Nothing about them is exceptional
but their place; caught out here so far
off the rails, they look a little spare,

at a loss even, but so do most
of the exhibits, for they *are* lost
in a special way. The use is gone, you see;
it isn't like Roman jewellery
or suchlike, for that could be in use
again; the owner's dead, not the purpose.

But what's here is as far obsolete
as only modern industry can get.
What it did is being better done,
or not at all. A discontinued line,
last week's Top Thirty, last year's video game.
It moves aimlessly in the same dream

as the facades of the dead businesses,
staring up the street with their empty eyes
at the new houses for the new people.

Things have moved on; things are unsentimental
like that. You can't force the world to need you,
and if it doesn't, there's nothing much to do

except wait civilly while a layer
of nostalgia distances you, like a picture
behind glass. There will be a curious grace
to your stance, out of context and purposeless
as it is; pointing the way back,
watching the litter left in the tide's track.

Pembrokeshire Seams

Wales is a process.
Wales is an artefact which the Welsh produce.
The Welsh make and remake Wales
day by day, year by year, generation after generation
if they want to.
          —Gwyn A. Williams

1.

Between Wiseman's Bridge and Saundersfoot

the coast path runs into coal wagon tunnels

and entrance holes drift down

into the base of a sheer cliff.

A pair of rails points from the path's edge

to launch the memory of themselves out over the bay

in perfect alignment with the next tunnel.

The children run on round: in the dark
there are hollows the shape of a body
they press themselves into. They
burst out at us like predictable ghosts
and we chase them into the light.

On the sand strip below us
the storm has flung a crop
of rotting star-fish.

2.

Those years I lived down here,
my parents let the bungalow to English visitors
and we spent the summers in two damp caravans.

We dug the garden patch for potatoes
and the hedge-bank would crumble
with dark shale, flaky stuff on its way
down the centuries to coal.
On a high fire you could coax it
to smoulder and flame.

3.

Coal was under us all the time,
the tail of the South Wales seam
surfacing again after the sea.
Shallow, tricky minings worked by families;
the men and children bunched like rats at the levels,
the women at a windlass winching up each
basket of good anthracite with a bent back.
Faults cracked and connived at the work—

this land never saw the rape of the valleys,
though the farmers' sons, worn by the rain
and sick of the smell of the shippen,
walked east and fed the deep pits and the iron.
On day trips their children's children
made their way back, built castles on the beach.

4.

My people—the Barrahs, the Thomases
raised cattle and potatoes
on good farming land from Llangwm to Jeffreyston.
Until my great-grandfather
that night in 1908
drunk and late from Narberth market,
roaring down the dark lanes, snapped his pony's leg
and turned the trap over his neck.
Six daughters, and a renegade son away in Canada,
saw the farm sold and split.

We lose ourselves down the years.

Under the earth at Jeffreyston,
wood groans, crack of the bones' cocoon.
A name smoothed away from the slant headstone.

5.

To the north, in the next county,
cottages are put to torch for the language,
for the idea of community.

A Range Rover coasts to the end of the lane;
shadows, murmurs, a burning bottle
clatters through mock-Georgian panes.
Rebecca rises to purify the tribe.

Not here; below the Landsker
we've been eased out of such extremes.

6.
It is a summer's day. The sea burns
against the eye.
A sky full of laughter and fat gulls.

On the boat to Caldey Island,
looking back you see the fields glint.
The windscreens on the cliff
pearl like standing water.
Deep down lanes a crop of caravans;
sites flower like clumps of nettles.

We trail our hands in the sea.
What did we imagine they would hold?
In the shock of cold they whiten
to the beauty of bones, of coral.

Midnights

An ice wind from the east razors across
the water, heaves and slams up our road. All night
our windows flinch and rattle with bitter complaints,
for hours the roof lifts and the attic breathes.

In the morning the last of our apples lie
bounced and bruised beneath the trees,
our front cherry's bare as a plucked chicken,
leaves downed across the lawn, its carcass full of sky.

A handful of slates, as old as the century
have snapped and slid to crash the sloping
panes of the verandah—slivers and blades
of glass in the flower border like dew glistening.

I bend for an hour over the job, filling
a bucket with needles, jags and shards.
This evening the weather man promises calm,
explains, last night's storm was brewed in Poland,

a wind from Warsaw chilling across the continent to Wales.
We hold to each other now
and listen to nothing but midnight
taxis speeding out of town.

As I stroke your arm
a glass sliver still in my finger
bloodies the two of us.
The windows' thin moonlight fails.

Jack Watts

squints across a sprouting field,
chews at a leaf, then weighs your crop
to the nearest bag.

Soft cap down to the eyes
and what had been somebody's suit
held by bailing cord;
he is pigmented with dirt
as if washing would have drained
away the year's knowledge.

The whole county waits:
in April the Pembrokeshire Earlies come
a stiff, dark green out of the ground.
Jack and his tribe pour
like Winter rats from their cottage.

Jack stops at the stile,
pushes the cap back to the perch of his head,
then walks along a row to what becomes
the centre of the field.
He delivers a potato from the earth,
soil spilling from the web of tubers,
shaking from the clumps.
He scrapes through dirt and skin;
the sweet flesh goes between his leather lips,
a nugget lodging in the jags of his teeth.

He closes his eyes on the taste—
it is the soil crumbling, the crush
of frost, the rain carried in on the sea,
the sweat of planting.

He holds the ridged sweetness to his nose,
between finger and thumb it glistens,

the rarest egg, the first
potato and the last.

The Death of Richard Beattie-Seaman in the Belgian Grand Prix, 1939

Trapped in the wreckage by his broken arm
he watched the flames flower from the front end.
So much pain—*Holy Jesus, let them get to me*—
so much pain he heard his screams like music
when he closed his eyes—the school organ at Rugby
Matins with light slanting down
hot and heady from the summer's high windows.
Pain—his trousers welded by flame to his legs.
His left hand tore off the clouded goggles—
rain falling like light into the heavy trees,
the track polished like a blade.
They would get to him, they were all coming
all running across the grass, he knew.

The fumes of a tuned Mercedes smelt like
boot polish and tear gas—coughing, his screams rising
high out of the cockpit—high
away back to '38 *Die Nurburgring.*
He flew in with Clara
banking and turning the Wessex through a slow circle
over the scene—sunlight flashing off the line of cars,
people waving, hoardings and loudspeakers, swastikas
and the flags of nations lifted in the wind he stirred.
She held his arm tightly, her eyes were closed.

He felt strong like the stretched wing of a bird,
the course mapped out below him.
That day Lang and Von Brauchitsch and Caracciola
all dropped out and he did it—won
in the fourth Mercedes before a crowd of half a million
—the champagne cup, the wreath around his neck,
An Englishman the toast of Germany
The camera caught him giving a Hitlergruss.

Waving arms, shouts and faces, a mosaic
laid up to this moment—La Source—tight—the hairpin
the trees—tight—La Source—keeping up the pace
Belgium—La Source hairpin too tight.

With the fire dying, the pain dying
the voices blurred beneath the cool licks of rain.
To be laid under the cool sheets of rain.
A quiet with, just perceptible, engines roaring
as at the start of a great race.

· INTERVIEW WITH MEIC STEPHENS ·

DL: How did you first become interested in poetry?

MS: I began writing verse and reading modern poetry during my last year at secondary school. I continued to do so as an undergraduate at the U.C.W. Aberystwyth, where I edited *Dragon*, the college magazine, in 1961. I also contributed to *Universities' Poetry*, an annual anthology by students at British universities. I spent 1959–60 in France and 1961–62 training to be a teacher at Bangor, where I met Anthony Conran[1] and talked to him about poetry. I read French at university, and my academic training in English was confined to three years of studying it as a subsidiary subject. I think all this served to give me a non-English approach to Welsh writing in English.

In the autumn of 1962 I settled in Merthyr Tudful. Harri Webb was a big influence on me there—and I on him. In those days I was a very active member of Plaid Cymru. I stood as a candidate in Merthyr at the General Election of 1966; no, I wasn't elected.

DL: What was the publishing scene in Wales like prior to your founding of *Poetry Wales* in 1965?

MS: We were very few in number who had any interest in what we called Anglo-Welsh literature in 1962, and there was no English-language "publishing scene" in Wales. I was encouraged in my endeavors not only by Harri Webb, Tony Conran and Gerald Morgan, but by several eminent Welsh-speakers such as Aneirin Talfan Davies and Jac L. Williams, who gave favorable attention to *Poetry Wales* in the Welsh-language press.

My first attempt as a publisher, under the imprint of the Triskel Press, was *Triad* (1963), a booklet of poems by Harri Webb, Peter M. Griffith (now Gruffydd), and myself. It sold five hundred copies, mainly to Plaid Cymru people, in less than a year. I went on to publish Gerald Morgan's paperback, *The Dragon's Tongue* (1966), and then pamphlets in the Triskel Poets series by John Tripp, Herbert Williams, and Leslie Norris, and a few other smaller items.

DL: What were some of the obstacles you faced when setting up a poetry magazine in Wales at that time?

MS: Some practical considerations. When I launched *Poetry Wales* in May, 1965, I printed five hundred copies and paid the printer £47. As I had no subsidy and no financial backing, I sold copies directly myself and relied on friends in the ranks of Plaid Cymru to sell copies for me, rather than go through the shops. The first number quickly sold out, as did subsequent numbers, except that I received a grant (£10 per number, I think it was) from the Welsh Committee of the Arts Council of Great Britain, as it then was. The administrative chores I did myself, but by the time the second number appeared I was married and had the help of my wife. I don't think it is generally realized how heavy the administrative burden of running a magazine usually is, and many have been put off by it, but I enjoyed it. I still have the accounts for the Triskel Press, together with notebooks and scrapbooks showing details of its affairs.

DL: What were some of the models to which you referred when setting up the magazine and press? Were similar literary endeavors in Scotland or Ireland in your mind?

MS: I took my title from *Poetry Ireland* and was also aware of some of the magazines associated with the poets of the Scottish Renaissance, Hugh MacDiarmid in particular. But I had also read Keidrych Rhys's *Wales* and Gwyn Jones's *Welsh Review* and, of course, *The Anglo-Welsh Review*, which was the only other English-language Welsh magazine in existence at the time.

My aim, as editor of *Poetry Wales*, was to provide an opportunity for poets to publish their work and to create an audience for them, as a contribution to the fostering of a Welsh literary culture in English. I saw this in a wider political context—the rendering articulate of the English-speaking Welsh (to put it rather grandly), and their participation in their country's affairs. I had no party political motives—I was not a traditional nationalist primarily concerned with the Welsh language—but I realized and hoped that *Poetry Wales* might become a conduit for a consciousness of Wales through the English language.

DL: English magazines and reviewers have been paying a bit more attention to Welsh and Anglo-Welsh writing in the last decade than previously, though not so much as the writing deserves. Can you comment on why this might be happening?

MS: I should like to reply that it doesn't matter much what English writers or critics say about Welsh writing in English and I sometimes do when I read an ill-informed review in the English journals. But the truth is that we need to have attention paid to us from outside Wales occasionally, if only to "see ourselves as others see us." It also helps, Wales being the place it is, with regard to media coverage, book sales, and the syllabus. I suppose it's inevitable that most attention will be paid to writers like Dylan Thomas, David Jones, and R. S. Thomas, but I wish some of our better younger writers were taken more seriously in England.

DL: What is the quality of critical commentary on Anglo-Welsh writing in the literary magazines of Wales? Are there difficulties and advantages specific to Wales in terms of creating a productive critical environment?

MS: I think it's far more important that we should be able to read regular reviews of Anglo-Welsh writing in our own magazines, and in this respect the three main journals—*Poetry Wales, Planet,* and the *New Welsh Review*—play an essential role. I think the standard of criticism, on the whole, is good—with occasional lapses, but then that is a healthy sign. One of the difficulties is that most writers and critics in Wales are acquainted with one another, and tend to don kid gloves when dealing with one another's work. Among the things I miss is a long-term, passionately argued debate about literature or critical theory and the emergence of opposing camps. But perhaps Wales, or the literary community in Wales, is too small for that. We have, after all, only a few excellent critics—as distinct from writers who write reviews—and they tend to be limited in their interests by their academic training.

DL: Could you describe the advantages and drawbacks of supporting literary magazines with public monies? Are there some dangers inherent in the Arts Council grant-giving system (including the idea of bursaries for writers)?

MS: None of the existing English-language magazines could survive without subsidy. I do not believe that the Arts Council has ever interfered with the editorial process—it never did in my time, anyway. The main danger is that, in cushioning the magazine against financial loss, the Council's subsidies can have the effect of discouraging initiative in selling the magazines. The whole question of distribution and sales remains problematic, and there is little evidence that the publishers have begun to tackle this problem. I sometimes think there is, anyway, only a limited audience for the literary magazines and that we shouldn't worry too much about sales as long as they are not going down. The sad fact is that not all writers, or would-be writers, buy the magazines. For example, I understand that only about a third of the members of the Welsh Academy take the *New Welsh Review*, which is published under the society's aegis. And if the thousands of people who would like to see their work in print would only buy the magazines occasionally, the need for subsidy would be much less, or the income could be used to pay editors and contributors something like a professional fee.

DL: Currently, Wales has three major English-language literary magazines: *Poetry Wales*, primarily for poetry; *New Welsh Review* for poetry, fiction, and criticism; and *Planet* for poetry, fiction, and social/cultural commentary. Is there a different kind of English-language magazine that you would like to see?

MS: I would like to see a more frequent tabloid magazine, with a smaller retail price, perhaps a monthly, carrying verse, short stories, and news, that could be sold in schools and colleges and at literary events. I would also like to read a serious literary magazine with a Welsh editorial point of view, more selective than the others and not hankering after a wide circulation, not trying to do everything but devoted to the fostering of a specifically Welsh literature in English, and well informed about what's happening elsewhere. Perhaps I will start one or the other some day!

DL: How do you account for the success of publishing in Wales in terms of the quantity and quality of writing, especially poetry, that is currently being published?

MS: I don't think there would be much publishing of literature in Wales if it was not for subsidy from Government sources—the Welsh Office and the county councils via the Welsh Books Council and the Welsh Arts Council. The whole system depends on subsidy, without which it would collapse. At the same time, presses like Gomer (and formerly Llyfrau'r Dryw/Christopher Davies) have tried to operate as commercial publishers, with some success; but they depend on other work as printers for their bread and butter; they too are dependent as publishers on government subsidy. As for Seren and Barddas, they were heavily subsidized from the start, and it seems unlikely that they will ever be commercial publishers in this sense.

DL: How does the Arts Council influence, directly or indirectly, the quality, quantity, or genre of writing produced in Wales? Has the Arts Council deliberately encouraged publication of poetry over prose, or are specific cultural conditions involved?

MS: The Literature Committee of the Arts Council, when I was Literature Director, often discussed the need to stimulate the writing of prose, and several initiatives were taken. The bursary scheme, for example, was primarily intended to help prose writers. It is largely a question of time and commitment on the writer's part. Quite a few good novels were written with the help of the bursaries, and many prizes went to novelists. It is not that the Council deliberately encouraged publication of poetry: it was just that there were always more poets seeking publication than novelists. In Wales, poetry has always been at the heart of the literary tradition, while the novel is a comparatively recent genre.

DL: Could you speak about some of the changes or trends that occurred during your time at the Arts Council?

MS: It was in 1967 that Literature was admitted to the Royal Charter of the Arts Council of Great Britain; previously the Council's support for literature, mainly poetry, had been small and intermittent. The Welsh Committee of the Arts Council had done little for Literature in Wales before 1967. In that year the Committee became the Welsh Arts Council and the Literature Department was formed. I was the first Literature Director and, as the officer of the Literature Committee, I had responsibility for creating the Council's policies for Literature, and for implementing them. The three areas in which the results of the Council's work were clearly to be seen were in its support for writers—bursaries, prizes, payment; in publication—magazines and books; in public access—readings, societies, the Oriel Bookshop, and so on. The WAC allocation to Literature in 1967 was £18,000 and in 1990 it was about £850,000. I think it fair to say that I played a major part in transforming the situation, but I must leave it to others to say precisely how. There may be an M.A. in it for someone!

DL: There has been a lot of controversy in Wales about the number of settlers coming from England, especially into areas that have been Welsh-language strongholds. Are there ways in which this potential audience might affect publishing in Wales?

MS: I think there is a need for more books in English which explain, interpret and reflect the Welsh culture, aimed at English-speaking incomers. It's likely that some already make efforts to read such books but, alas, they are probably very few.

DL: A number of writers have taken a stance against Anglo-Welsh literature, seeing it as a poor cousin to English literature and/or politically suspect (given the precarious position of Welsh-language culture and literature). What do you think about such a stance?

MS: I have always thought Anglo-Welsh—or Welsh Writing in English—one of the literatures of Wales, just as English is one of the languages. It has been my hope that a national literature in English might be created in Wales, in which all its people—Welsh and English speakers—would take an interest. The danger is that instead of being national, this writing might become provincial—looking to England for themes, styles, and approval—or so like literature in English that its Welsh characteristics are difficult or impossible to define. But it need not be so.

DL: What are some of the weaknesses and strengths in the work of the younger Anglo-Welsh poets? Are there ways in which they differ from their elders, such as Harri Webb or Glyn Jones?

MS: Anglo-Welsh poetry went through a "nationalist" phase in the 1960s. I never thought it would continue to do so, at least not at that strength. I wanted there to be a variety of modes, including the nationalist, and that's what we're beginning to have now. The variety may not be wide enough, but it's a start. I should be glad if another poet with Glyn Jones's knowledge of Welsh poetry, or Harri Webb's political convictions, were to emerge, and it's probably only a matter of time before he or she does. I am all for young Welsh poets being open to influences from abroad (if they are able), but at the same time we need to understand what it is that makes Welsh writing in English Welsh. This will probably be a continuing problem, as it is in Scotland and Ireland.

I am aware that some young Welsh poets are not a bit interested in "Welshness": poets, after all, are a selfish lot, and they show an interest only if they can draw some advantage. But they should remember that if it were not for the nationalist revival in the 1960s and the community of interest which has grown since then, they might not have a literary context in which to write now.

DL: During the last decade many more women writers are being published in Wales. Did the Arts Council play a role in encouraging publication of women?

MS: The Arts Council responded, as it should, to the growing interest in women's writing by helping to initiate competitions, anthologies, and even the publishing imprint Honno. This, by the way, was a special concern of mine, and I always found the Literature Committee sympathetic to it.

DL: Could you make any predictions about the future of Welsh writing in English?

MS: For me, the main question remains whether Welsh writing in English is going to become more Welsh—more concerned with Wales, its people, their history and their present condition. I have played my part in helping to create a national literature in English, from deep personal conviction, and it is known which side I am on.

▪ CATHERINE FISHER ▪

St Tewdric's Well

Toad on the soft black tarmac knows it's there;
screened by deadnettle, tumbled with ivy.
He enters the water like a devotee,
annointed with bubbles.

If you lean over, your shadow shrouds him;
dimly your eyes find watersnails
down on the deep green masonry, and coins,
discarded haloes.

Tewdric's miracle, not even beautiful,
slowly effacing itself in exuberant nettles,
its only movement the slow clouds,
the sun's glinting ascension.

Lost in the swish of grasses, the hot road,
blown ladybirds, soft notes from a piano;
and over the houses the estuary grey as a mirror,
its islands stepping-stones for Bran or Arthur.

Snake-bite

Today is the day she will shed her skin;
she does not know it.
On fabric flowers butterflies alight;
long, cool-tongued grasses lick her heels,
tantalise basking
fingers, supine in sunlight.

This is the day the film will fall
from her eyes, as the wind passes,
rustling its insinuation
to the blind blue skies,
and zig-zag flickers of ochre
fleck the green uneasy grasses.

Soon she will cast it aside, the old,
split, papery wrapping;
through the red heat behind the eyelid, drift
and drone of wasps,
the subtlest beast of all the field
is bringing its bright gift.

And maybe today she will start again;
slough off old vagaries,

burst constriction, full colour,
glisten, breathe, move with ease.
The grasses whisper. And look,
her eyes are open.

Immrama

First there was the island of the darkness.
When we rowed from there
the light was desolation for us.

And I remember a house with a golden chessboard
where we played too long.
What we lost I cannot remember.

As you go on it gets harder. Each landfall
an awakening of sorrows,
guile or treachery, the enticement of pleasures.

I lost my brother at the house of feathers,
good men at the harper's table.
There are always those who would hold us back.

You get used to the voices, the clinging fingers;
in every port the warning
'Beyond here is nothing but the sea'.

Islands of glass, islands of music and berries,
the isle of the locked door,
citadels and beaches where we dared not land,

these are behind us. Daily, the delirium rises;
it may be that smudge
on the horizon is a trick of my eyes.

And would we know that land if we should find it?
They say the scent of apples
wafts on the water; there is honey, hum of bees,

salmon leap into the boat. They say the others,
the lost ones, laugh on the sand.
But behind them, who are those strangers crowding the cliffs?

Rubbish

The rubbish bags were still
outside the council offices last night.
Ogwr Labour councillor
Dilwyn Davies said he had been
on holiday
in Spain
and knew nothing
"Go away and put up
with the buggers who've gone with you,
pissing in the corridors all night, letting
off fire extinguishers,
trying to kick in your door.
F. off back home to your island
like the Guardia tell you
and find this. It's the Nats,

someone ought to put them down."

The Western Mail told of
"Thirty stinking bags, most of them carrying CYMRU stickers"
Local shops had sold out,
"mostly to families ashamed to be English.
They put the stickers on their boots when
they go abroad and pretend to be us."

It's a quiet place Wales, no violence.
Who died in the Falklands without fighting?
Who couldn't march and had to turn back?
"The demoralisation culminated in a disgraceful panic
during which many of them seemed quite incapable
of understanding, or unwilling to carry out the simplest order."

There is nothing to fear from the acquiescing taffs
chuck them a few pecuniary scraps and
they'll bow to the ground.

At Penrhys in the Rhondda
they've built a new youth centre
with no windows. Walls that can't
be scarred by the hapless unemployed.

In Cardiff the Clifton St. jewellers
opposite the police station has been broken into
five times. Most recently thieves avoided
the new £200 metal grills protecting windows
by taking off the slates and coming in
through the roof.

At Porthcawl local authority workers cancelled a Max Boyce
concert by blocking the entrances with
refuse. Traders warn of a health
hazard. There is talk of a people's backlash.
The ruling Labour group will press on
with their plans to build new
council offices on a promontory at Southerndown.
"Like a Twentieth-Century Iron-Age fort,"
enthused the architect, "can only be
picketed from one side. On all
others will just be the sea."

"But these aren't the Welsh," said Mr Davies
from his armchair at 43 Blaencwm Road
(he can't use his office, it's still full of trash)
"these are the interlopers, tinkers, Irish, English,
three generations and they think they own the place.
They're even making their kids learn the
language now the whole thing's too late."

Mr Davies thinks a firm from Birmingham will
shift the refuse.
Prestostik, Luton, have reprinted CYMRU stickers
in exact replicas of GB plates. For
emphasis is added the translation
PAYS DE GALLES in italic face.

At Penrhys the workless have followed the capital
and scaled the drainpipes.
The youth club's light domes
now lie in fragments

on the unfinished floor
beneath.

The Speaker

At the lectern
the speaker gestures
moves his hands
sends his arms in circles.
He is aware that his hairy trousers
are too tight at the crotch.
He would like to dance, you think,
but he must follow his script.
He looks up
rubs his forehead, flicks his ear,
pulls his chin, smooths his hair,
he winds his watch,
shakes his papers,
there is no drinking water
he wants to cough.

>My script writer advocated
>constantly cleaning the teeth. Two
>torch bulbs either side of the back
>molars and a nickel cadmium cell under
>each arm.

Smile.

The speaker stares
he has lost his place.

The page is a maze
of text and space.

He looks up
it is the wrong moment
there are empty chairs
dozers, shufflers,
whisperers, yawners,
banging doors,
barking dogs.

The answer is rote
learn the script
show the teeth
throw the voice
strepsils, flouride mouthwash,
plaque tablets, Sensodyne gum cream,
small mirrors on the ends of sticks.

At the interval
the organizer explains
there are usually more people than this
last month we had a science fiction writer,
he was a big draw, it's the rain,
wrong night, all the posters we put up,
but they'll come later, they always come,
bang and clack, you won't mind,
it's no interruption, let them in,
but it really ought to be better than this.

And upstairs the three who have showed

queue for the toilet
while the organizer phones for a room
and finds them all booked.

The speaker is alone in the auditorium
he has fixed his pants with Sellotape
he shuffles his papers, clears his throat,
he wants to start the second half.
The audience, who thought he'd finished,
have gone
the organizer explains with a nervous laugh,
the doortake was low, can they post the fee?
The speaker nods, sod it,
writing is such a prolific art
at times you can't even give it away free.

cars

they used to mend cars in our street
all of them   shammying headlamps
draining sumps   fat terry with a
jaguar walnut leather spanners
engine parts laid out on the pavement like art
mr brown thirteen years exorcising rust
from a faded citroen   the manzarettis
faking speed bolting chrome
onto family saloons   gone

in the new world   this one
where the heart is invisible   the

pavements are solid with white skirted
coupes shining they start everytime

I park in the next street run to work
I am always running   the next task is
always more important than this one   arrive
as fast as I can   I know
none of the owners   coats   hats   important
things on their faces   mine is empty
or inscrutable   standing on the front
path with a foam-loaded car brush
wondering breathlessly where now   the
family no longer live here   clean spaces   ghosts
couldn't make it go   yesterday   rain   terry
would have given me a lift   the bus
runs from somewhere I've never been before

are we rich   my son asks me   I tell him no   no no
not yet.

Block

when you don't you can't
when you can't you say you could
you could but you don't
you don't, but oh you would
you would if you could but it's hard
and if it's hard it hurts
and if it hurts then you don't
but you don't say you don't.

You say you would; yes—
you say you would, you would
but of course you don't
and that's bad when you don't.
I had an uncle once who never did
he never did, ever did,
he couldn't because he didn't
he didn't start so when he wouldn't
he said he didn't because he never did.
My uncle really couldn't, no really,
he said I can't because I don't
I won't because I'm not
and if I did then you wouldn't
because I'd've done it first
and better naturally
and you wouldn't want to, would you,
after that.
Good boy my uncle,
wrote novels
never put a ship inside
a bottle in his life.

· HILARY LLEWELLYN-WILLIAMS ·

Birch

December 24–January 20

After Twelfth Night comes the reality
of winter. When the greenery's stripped down
it's barefaced, blowing under the door.
Mean days dragging out a fraction more
before dark, make our myth of spring
ridiculous. I walk out into the stark
endless moment of January.

Old snow slumps in the hedge,
stretching from the fields
wet to the birchwood, raw
black tangle against the grey.
Mud ruts, brown ice under my boot
snaps and seeps as I trudge up

to the sad ranks of trees, the thin
skin birches in their thaw.

These brittle twigs swept clear of leaves
whipping along the light,
points of dark bud concealing green,
I'll tie a bundle to my broom, for flight:
no shelter here, the rain falls through
this frostwood, the sky stares between.
The bramble jags, the stag horns of the scrub
bad musk of leafmould, in the dusk
that stirs behind my shoulder.

Birch stems lean to the loud stream
crowding beneath the wind,
thrashing their rods at winter stumps,
at the cracked, dimwit days.
Think of the woods brushed with a green haze.

Think of the covered hills
filling with cleaner light, and a gap
in the clouds for something to glance through.
I stoop in a cold shade
gathering twigs for a journey.

The Cruellest Month

April 1986

This long, cold spring, this refusal
of growth and heat: just a few bitter weeds

clenched hard on the ground, and rain
gone brutal, slubbed with sleet. We all
look desperate. Our eyes are wide and white
from watching the news, our faces shut and grey
against the weather. Snow on the high ground.
The last days—it feels like the last days:
a summer we have longed for, that never comes;
life shrunk back in on itself. Crows feeding
close to the house. Children kept in, subdued,
backs to a blear window. Waiting. Waiting.

If spring would come, if the future would only come
to relieve the present, these familiar gales
blowing from town to town; if the post should bring
those long-awaited letters; if the world
should suddenly get sick of itself, and change—
but there's no change, only wind from the north-east
gusting day after day. It's like the end
of innocence, those simple former years
when summer followed winter, when the young
grew up to adulthood in the old way,
looked forward to it. Now the fighting planes
take off, like birds of doom. Come summer, come.

To the Islands

Driving to Llanybydder from the hills
in sunlight, a clean blue sky
bathing us in its image: a light-pocket,
an open eye in all those weeks of rain,

we suddenly saw the sea in a strange place,
inland. We followed a new coast:
pale lucid water filled the low ground
to the west, and risen islands stood

netted with fields or thinly brushed
with trees, and shoreside cottages
whitewashed, perched over a harbour—
a landscape from the inner Hebrides

exact and stunning. Though of course we knew
it was only a trick of mist, sucked up
from unremarkable sodden earth, still
we cried out happily: "Look at the sea!"

So it shall be someday, when the polar ice
melts, and expanding oceans lift
over the land again. Sea licking
these hills into islands and promontories

the Teifi swallowed into a sea-loch
and lush farms drowned, and hill-farms turned
into fishermen's cottages. We could see
the future in a bowl of clear water,

seeing the present too, scrying the land
that is always there but mostly invisible—
the land's other face, the place where boats
put out from curved inlets, and green fields

tilt down to the sea; where eels thread
their way between tall hedges. Sun low
behind us, as far south as it will go
as we ran into the outer blurs of mist

and the islands vanished. Above, we sensed
the summer colour of sky without seeing it:
and, turning west, we crossed the plain grey river
in silence, like driving through water.

Brynberllan

This is a place where nothing really grows
but water: water and stones.

And concrete bungalows, and lost holdings.

Tilt of water from the mountainside
pushes under the road, and stones grow
overnight in our gardens: rainbuffed hard
perennials. We're on the flank
of the wind, even in summer.

But years ago, this was an apple orchard.

Rows and patterns of trees, all the way
down to the stream called *Comely*;
mossy barked, their darkblue stems at dusk,
the sun spread white at dawn on slopes
of blossom; warm air, stirred thick

with honey. Humming and swarms, and then
the smell of ripe fruit: those small
sharp western apples.

Crowded faces, bushels and basketfuls.

Everyone there, at work in the branches,
measuring the loads, brownarmed
and busy. Shouts in the crisp leaves.
Children rolling windfalls down the hill.
Foxes nosing at night through bruised grass.

And apple smoking in the soul-fires.

I think the traffic worsens year by year
just passing through. Rain's harsher too:
laced with acid and caesium, it fills
the stream called *Comely* and the stream
called *Blossom*. Nothing flourishes.

Yet sometimes we'll distill, between breath

and breath, a taste of sweetness:
yes, even now, a rustling of leaves
a blossom-drift. Between low flakes
of October sunlight, treeshapes flicker;
and evenings to the West bring cloud-landscapes
rising like a range of wooded hills,
a place of apple-orchards. Not here: beyond

reach, elsewhere, forsaken, forfeited.

Nola

In my childhood, I thought nothing existed beyond Vesuvius.
—De Immenso

Now I understand, I understand everything.
Bird's eggs are small pieces of sky;
the chicks inside are stolen from the wind

and the wind blows because the trees move it
with their dancing leaves: they move the lake too
into waves. And I know where night is made:

in the lake, from black stones in the mud there.
Dark breathes out and rises from the water,
and daylight every morning moves the leaves.

In those trees by the river, mothers find their babies;
I've seen them walking into the woods with baskets
on windy afternoons. Today I helped Mamma

pick bilberries. She said I'm sharp as a bird.
I know about angels, too: they live in the Sun,
but they visit Nola sometimes secretly

streaming down in bars of light—they look like specks
but they're really huge, huge. Here's my cave
where I talk to them, and leave them figs and flowers:

in the morning there's nothing left, so I know they love me.
Can you see that dark hump where the world ends?
We call it Vesuvius, the shadow mountain;

nobody lives there, it's too black and cold—
not like our green mountain, with goats and sheep
and Uncle Taddeo's hut, and the white track

up to the summer pasture. There's our holy well
with its chained cup, and light in the water
rolling around like a snake to make you strong.

And I have discovered bee-swarms in the earth:
I've heard them when I lie in the June grass
on hot still days, humming under my head,

under my hands, down in the earth's hive—
or is it the world buzzing? That deep, thick honey voice,
her soil, her stones, alive. See! I understand.

The Inner Artificer

Man labours on the surface of things; but Nature works from within.
—De Causa

The scientist's posed in a pigsty—
an awkward smile on his round foolish face—
with his creature, transgenic monster, poor pig,
blind, bloated and arthritic, a coarse slab.
That smile of hesitant triumph,
those well-scrubbed fingers touching the prone
thick body in the straw, show no remorse;
more a coy, teasing promise, an allure.

And I wonder, Bruno, what you'd think of him
that gene-magician in his white coat,

his surface-work. They still say *Mother Nature*—
meaning a woman, weak and pliable,
limited, passive, open to be explored,
discarded, raped. Mother gives more and more.

But among us, *da noi*, Nature is called
the inner artificer. And she's everywhere,
strong, steadfast: power in the womb
of matter, the spirit that shines
through things. She's a voice
heard in a room, sounding to each corner,
everywhere resonant; we can't turn from her.

And she returns us our filth, feeds us
our stored-up poison. She will not spare
the seals, or our children. Deserts balloon,
malignant. As we divide, negate,
reduce and separate, she multiplies,
joins and reshapes the world, swarms out
from the core. She is not sentimental.

This grinning alchemist plays with the parts,
blind to the whole. Like his pig
he is paralyzed, stuck, sterile. He believes
in the old, flat, static Earth. He believes in Hell.

While Nature still works from the centre,
expelling galaxies, singing through every door.
Revolutionary Queen of the chromosomes,
the inner artificer. Hidden and sure.

Flotsam

The marriage of wood and water
    spawned this creature:
wood chromosomes and water chromosomes
    juggled together

shaping a wizened femur
    as if old ivy-woman tossed her legbone
to the elements, and the waves took it

to scour the moss and the dirt away,
then rolled it back to the shore.

There are faces in it, gargoyles, girnings,
    the grin of a running dog:
an ivy-dog running from tree to tree,
    a sea-dog cocking its leg

at the suck-slick of the tide
    that whittled it
by the push and pull of the moon;

wood and water and the lunar carver
    conjuring a fake, a changeling
brat, a beglamoured stock
    outwardly whole

but inwardly skewed like this.
    I'd love to see the rest
of the skeleton: the ribcage opening

its shrivelled petals, the pelvis writhing
in exuberant loops, the skull—

what would they make of the skull? The one
    true giveaway, that careful smoothing of flesh
cannot disguise. And of course it was
    by the eyes you knew them inhuman.

The goblin urge to recreate, to play
    with blocks of DNA, to make believe:
and we're part of the game

so an ivy stem can mimic a thigh bone
and our veins web out like a tree

with the sea moving in rhythm
    through us, casting us back
along with other flotsam, woodbones and shells
    in the tidal reaches

and who
    comes combing the beaches for what remains of us?

· R. S. THOMAS ·

FROM *COUNTERPOINT*, "BC"

No, in the beginning was silence
that was broken by the word
forbidding it to be broken.

Hush: the sound of a bird landing
on water; sound of a thought
on time's shore; practice of Ur-language

by the first human. An echo
in God's mind of a conceived
statement. The sound of a rib

being removed out of the side
of the androgynous hero. The mumbling
of the Host by reptilian

lips. The shivering of love's
mirror as truth's frost
begins mercilessly to take hold.

■   ■   ■

If he had not given them stone
how could they have begun building?

Without his shadow to measure his height
by Babel would have been a word long.

Does a God sleep? On that first night
the stars blinked ubiquitously as his eyelids.

How could they know, the first farmers,
the sowing of corn was the sowing of armed men?

■   ■   ■

I want . . . Help me. Listen . . . I—
no time. What is life but
deciduous? That I in my day, no
other . . . I, I, I, before the world,
in the present tense; so, now,
here, stating my condition—
whose else? Not my fault; I
at the centre, everything else
echoes, reflections. What is water
but mirror, air but returner
of the personal cadenza I . . .

I . . . I—What is my name?
I, a pacifist, fighting in the dark-
ness against the will not to be.
There will be no peace in the world
so long as the angel resists me.

■　　■　　■

There is a being, they say,
neither body nor spirit,
that is more power than reason, more reason
than love, whose origins
are unknown, who is apart
and with us, the silence
to which we appeal, the architect
of our failure. It takes the genes
and experiments with them and our children
are born blind, or seeing have
smooth hands that are the instruments
of destruction. It is the spoor
in the world's dark leading away
from the discovered victim, the expression
the sky shows us after
an excess of spleen. It has gifts it
distributes to those least fitted
to use them. It is everywhere and
nowhere, and looks sideways into the shocked face
of life, challenging it to disown it.

FROM *COUNTERPOINT,* "INCARNATION"

Was there a resurrection?
Did the machine put its hand
in man's side, acknowledging lordship?

There was a third day and
a third year and the sepulchre
filled up with humanity's bones.

Was this where a god died?
Was Nietzsche correct, the smell
of oil the smell of corruption also?

On the skyline I have seen gantries
with their arms out awkwardly
as love and money trying to be reconciled.

FROM *COUNTERPOINT,* "CRUCIFIXION"

Silent, Lord,
as you would have us be,
lips closed, eyes swerving aside
towards the equation:
$x + y^2 = y + x^2$?
It does not balance.
What has algebra to do
with a garden? Either
they preceded it or came
late. The snake's fangs
must have been aimed

at a calculable angle
against a possible refusal
of the apple of knowledge.
Was there a mathematics
before matter to which
you were committed? Or is it
man's mind is to blame,
spinning questions out of itself
in the infinite regress?
It is we gave the stars names,
yet already the Zodiac
was in place—prophesying,
reminding? The Plough
and Orion's Sword eternally
in contradiction. We close
our eyes when we pray
lest the curtain of tears
should come down on a cross
being used for the first time to prove
the correctness of a negation.

FROM *COUNTERPOINT*, "AD"

We must reverse our lenses.
Too often we have allowed them
to lead us into a dark past.
Looking through the right
end, we see how that dawn
had the brightness of flowers.
It is the future is dark
because one by one

we are removing these paintings
from our exhibition. We walk
between blank walls, scrawled
over with the graffiti
of a species that has turned its gaze
back in, not to discover
its incipient wings, but the slime
rather and the quagmire from which
it believes itself to have emerged.

■   ■   ■

It is one of those faces
beginning to disappear
as though life were at work
with its eraser. It drizzles
at the window through which
I regard it. As one realising
its peril, it accosts me
in silence at every corner
of my indifference, appealing
to me to save it gratuitously
from extinction. There was a moment
it became dear to me, a skull
brushed by a smile as the sun
brushes a stone through ravelled
passages in the hill mist.
Must I single it with a name?
I am coming to believe,
as I age, so faithful its attendance
upon the eye's business, it is myself

I court; that this face, vague
but compelling, is a replica
of my own face hungry for meaning
at life's pane, but blearing it
over as much with my shortness
of faith as of breath.

■　　■　　■

'The body is mine and the soul is mine'
says the machine. 'I am at the dark source
where the good is indistinguishable
from evil. I fill my tanks up
and there is war. I empty them
and there is not peace. I am the sound,
not of the world breathing, but
of the catch rather in the world's breath.'

Is there a contraceptive
for the machine, that we may enjoy
intercourse with it without being overrun
by vocabulary? We go up
into the temple of ourselves
and give thanks that we are not
as the machine is. But it waits
for us outside, knowing that when
we emerge it is into the noise
of its hand beating on the breast's
iron as Pharisaically as ourselves.

■　　■　　■

On an evening like this
the furies have receded.
There are only the shining sentinels
at hand: Yeats in his tower,
who was his own candle,
poring over the manuscript
of his people, discovering pride
in defeat; discovering the lidless
eye that beholds the beast
and the virgin. Edward Llwyd,
finding the flower that grew
nowhere but in Wales,
teaching us to look for rare things
in high places. Owain Glyndŵr
who tried blowing that flower
into flame in the memory
of an oppressed nation. The poets,
all of them, in all languages,
pausing on their migration
between thought and word
to watch here with me now
the moon come to its fifteenth phase
from whose beauty and madness
men have withdrawn these last days,
hand on heart, to its far
side of sanity and darkness.

R.I.P.

1588–1988

And the Englishman asks:
How do you say it? twitching
his nostril at the odiousness
of comparisons between a Welsh
village and capital of the world
as instruments of salvation.

It is off the main road
even to market; nothing to induce
the traveller to a digression
but rumours of the tumbling
of water out of the sky
copiously as grace pouring

to irrigate the hearts
of a people that had grown arid
as much from the law's bones
they were fed on, as from
the anarchy on their borders
desiccating charity in its east wind.

If he was incumbent,
there was a responsibility also
incumbent upon him.

The river was the mill—
water turning his pen
to the grinding of Hebrew

to Welsh corn, now flooding
him with vocabulary,
now smooth enough for the dancing

of his mind's fly time
and again on its surface,
angling for the right word.

We are inheritors
of his catch. He invested
his haul, so readers to come

should live off the interest.
Imagine his delight
in striking those Welsh nouns,

as they rose from the shadows,
that are alive as ever
stippling the book's page.

It was not always success.
The hills are high; asking their question
too sharply, they met the iciness
of a reply. Language can be
like iron. Are we sure we can bend
the Absolute to our meaning?

When the moon rises, beautiful
and indifferent, its reflection
in windows is as of his face
staring from an asylum of thought.

To be so near, and to be as far off
as Andromeda; this is torment.

　　History has no camera,
　　so his photograph waits
　　on the imagination. Let
　　me take it for you,

　　unemphatic about
　　features, but crinkling the lips
　　with Welsh humour at the thought
　　the book was to be used

　　for the promotion of English.
　　A face with irony's
　　inaudible laughter tickling
　　it: this is for your album.

Is an obsession with language
an acknowledgement we are too late
to save it? It has been infiltrated
already by daub and symbol.
We are graduates of the cartoon,
victims of the subliminal
coaxing of smiles and colours.
Now four hundred years in arrears
with our rent, we prefer a pilgrimage
to a birth-place, contributing generously
to a memorial, preparing to go
backward in time up long lanes,
through Welsh weather, to condescend

for an hour to listen to an outmoded
language's congratulation of itself.

In the beginning
was the word. What
word? At the end
is the dust. We know
what dust; the dust
that the bone comes to,
that is the fall-out
from our hubris, the
dust on the Book
that, out of breath
with our hurry
we dare not blow off
in a cloud, lest out
of that cloud should
be resurrected the one
spoken figure we have grown
too clever to believe in.

A Marriage

We met
        under a shower
of bird-notes.
        Fifty years passed,
love's moment
        in a world in
servitude to time.

She was young;
I kissed with my eyes
            closed and opened
them on her wrinkles.
            'Come' said death,
choosing her as his
            partner for
the last dance. And she,
            who in life
had done everything
            with a bird's grace,
opened her bill now
            for the shedding
of one sigh no
            heavier than a feather.

· NOTES ·

Notes to the poems provide brief explanations for lesser-known references, especially those relating to Welsh history and culture. Most are based on information provided by the authors.

INTRODUCTION

1. For an outline of the causes of decline, see Bud Khleif, *Language, Ethnicity and Education in Wales* (1980): 55–56. Other relevant sources include *Welsh in Education and Life* (1927), *The Welsh Language Today* (1973), and *The Welsh Language 1961–1981: An Interpretive Atlas* (1985).

2. See Brinley Thomas's "A Cauldron of Rebirth: The Industrial Revolution and the Welsh Language" in *The Industrial Revolution and the Atlantic Economy* (1993). Thomas argues that employment in the coal and steel industries of south Wales during the second half of the nineteenth century enabled Welsh speakers to avoid emigration to England or the United States.

3. The "best-loved programmes" on S4C "reach audiences of 100,000 on a Welsh-speaking base of half a million" (Elan Stephens, "View from the Quadrant," *Planet* 84: 30–33).

4. Many members of Cymdeithas yr Iaith Gymraeg have been imprisoned for their part in nonviolent acts of civil disobedience designed to test the 1967 Welsh Language Act.

5. Recently three men suspected of involvement with "Meibion Glyndŵr" ("Sons of Glyndŵr," a reference to Owain Glyndŵr, the leader of a fifteenth-century rebellion against English rule, known in English—especially through Shakespeare's *Henry V*—as Owen Glendower), were charged with conspiracy to cause explosions. One of the three, Siôn Aubrey Roberts, was also charged with possessing explosives and sending explosive devices through the mail. All were acquitted of conspiracy; Roberts was convicted of the explosives charges and sentenced to twelve years in prison.

6. See John Aitchison and Harold Carter's article, "The Welsh Language in 1991—A Broken Heartland and a New Beginning?" (*Planet* 97, February/March 1993: 3–10), for an analysis of language trends since 1981

and projections on the future of the Welsh language.

7. *The Cost of Strangeness* (1982): 35.

8. According to the *Oxford Companion to the Literature of Wales* (1986).

9. Referring to the term "Anglo-Welsh" in *Cymru or Wales?* (1992), R. S. Thomas argues that "hyphenisation is betrayal."

10. From the interview with Meic Stephens, p. 176.

11. In *R. S. Thomas: Selected Prose* (1986).

12. From *Ugain o Gerddi* (1949).

13. Translation by David Lloyd and Mair Lloyd.

JOHN DAVIES
FROM "THE VISITOR'S BOOK"

sonnet 1
back of the *gwt*: back of the line.

rugger: rugby.

sonnet 6
Idris Davies: a poet (1905–53) of the coal-mining valleys of south Wales, particularly associated with the Depression of the 1930s.

Viscount Tonypandy: George Thomas, a Labour member of Parliament for a Cardiff constituency, accepted elevation to the House of Lords.

sonnet 8
my father must have thought . . . : unlike the poet, his father spoke Welsh.

sonnet 11
'sham ghosts': from "Welsh Language," a poem by R. S. Thomas.

In Port Talbot
Keir Hardie: a miners' leader and founder of the Labour Party. He

was the first socialist member of Parliament to be returned from Wales (from the Merthyr Tudful constituency).

Bethanias: chapels.

Regrouping

Joe Washington: a spiritual leader of the Lummi tribe during the 1980s. The pow-wow mentioned here took place in Tacoma, Washington.

Farmland

the English-speaking sea: The setting is northeast Wales. While its coastal areas are English-speaking, like the poet, its hinterland speaks Welsh mainly, as does the poet's wife.

FROM "READING THE COUNTRY"

These sonnets were prompted partly by poems translated from the Welsh, whose titles have been retained.

Penmon

Ieuan Wyn: a Welsh-language poet living in Bethesda at the heart of the slate-quarrying area, a stronghold of the Welsh language.

Cwmorthin

Twll din pob Sais: literally, "Arseholes to all Englishmen," derived from a popular toast in Wales.

FWA: the Free Wales Army, a group associated with bombings in Wales during the 1960s.

Fires

This sonnet was written against the background of the arson campaign of Meibion Glyndŵr (Sons of Glyndŵr) from 1979 onwards, targeting second homes owned by English people in Welsh-speaking areas (see p. xx of the introduction). Owain Glyndŵr led a rebellion against the English crown from 1400 to 1413. The setting of the poem is Gwynedd, the county with the largest proportion of Welsh speakers, bounded in the east by the River Conwy and in the west by the Llŷn peninsula.

Hooson: I. D. Hooson (1880–1948), a Welsh-language poet.

GILLIAN CLARKE

Fires on Llŷn

the footprint of God: In a radio program R. S. Thomas used the warm but empty form of the hare as a metaphor for the presence or absence of God.

Enlli . . . the knuckle-bone / or vertebra of a saint: Legend tells that twenty thousand saints are buried on the island of Enlli (Bardsey).

Neighbours

golau glas: blue light.

Sheila na Gig at Kilpeck

One of the seventy stone carvings on the corbel of the well-preserved twelfth-century church at Kilpeck, Herefordshire, is a Sheila na gig: a grinning, grotesque female figure, her hands pulling open her vulva.

Llŷr

In the Second Branch of *The Mabinogi*, the father of Manawydan, Bendigeidfran (Bran), and Branwen. A prototype of Shakespeare's King Lear. In origin a Celtic god of the sea.

Blodeuwedd

In the Fourth Branch of *The Mabinogi*, Blodeuwedd was created from the flowers of the oak, broom, and meadowsweet. She was turned into an owl as a punishment for adultery.

INTERVIEW WITH GILLIAN CLARKE

1. Run by the Taliesin Trust, Tŷ Newydd is a residential writers' center in Llanystumdwy, north Wales.

2. Ieuan ap Swrdwal (fl. 1430–80) is often cited as the first Welsh poet to write in English (see *Anglo-Welsh Poetry 1480–1980*, ed. Raymond Garlick and Roland Mathias, 1982). Dafydd ap Gwilym (fl. 1320–70) is one of the greatest Welsh poets.

3. Titled "Imagine This," the film is part of the "Statements" Arts series produced by BBC 2 Wales.

NIGEL JENKINS

Castell Carreg Cennen

The title refers to a Welsh-built medieval castle in the old Welsh princedom of southwest Wales (Deheubarth), much battled over by the defending Welsh and invading English.

Brawdy: the site both of an RAF station and a United States submarine listening post which has been a focus of many antinuclear protests.

Snowdrops

Paviland: a cave on the Gower peninsula where, in 1823, Dr. William Buckland found a skeleton stained with red ochre, which had evidently been ritually buried. At least eighteen thousand years old, it represented (until recently) the oldest human bone find in Britain and has been referred to as the remains of the first known Welshman.

tlws yr eira . . . : The Welsh words in the poem all, in various ways, mean "snowdrop."

JEAN EARLE

Afterwards

pheromones: the delicate apparatus with which moths and butterflies detect each other's presence, often at a distance of miles.

Faithless Dreams
shift: work period, day or night.

her red dress: Dante and Beatrice met when both were children; she was wearing a red dress.

Old Tips
Tips are mountains of coal or slate waste, a result of mining.

Some tips were famed as wicked: in particular, the coal-tip at Aberfan, in south Glamorgan, which slid over Aberfan School in 1966, with the loss of all the teachers and most of the village children.

the annual sea: during depression in the mining industry, the only holiday for many children was the once-yearly chapel or church day trip to the sea.

Visiting Light
Rubbing with bluestone: a former custom in Wales (and parts of England) of scouring the wet step with a lump of stone.

OLIVER REYNOLDS
Dysgu
The title is the Welsh word for "learning."

Daearyddiaeth
The title is the Welsh word for "geography."

Hiraeth: Longing, especially for one's country.

Gwlad, gwlad: "country," "land." "Gwlad, gwlad" are the first two words of the Welsh National Anthem.

L.M.C. 1980
L. M. C.: Lewis Merthyr Colliery.

NCB: National Coal Board.

CHRIS BENDON

Swansea

The title refers to the second largest city in Wales.

the night raids of years ago: Swansea was severely bombed during the Second World War.

INTERVIEW WITH JEREMY HOOKER

1. John Stuart Williams and Meic Stephens, eds. (1969).

2. Rather than seeing Anglo-Welsh literature as a twentieth-century phenomenon with nineteenth-century roots, Garlick and Mathias argue that an identifiable Anglo-Welsh literature extends back at least to the fifteenth century.

3. *John Cowper Powys* in the Writers of Wales series (1973) and *John Cowper Powys and David Jones: a Comparative Study* (1979).

4. *Ten Anglo-Welsh Poets*, ed. Sam Adams (1974), includes just one woman, Gillian Clarke.

5. *Poetry Wales* magazine, founded by Meic Stephens in 1965, was instrumental in promoting a new generation of English-language poets in Wales. Seren Books is the premier publisher of English-language poetry in Wales. Roland Mathias contributed to the growth of Anglo-Welsh literature through his work as a poet, critic, editor, and anthologist.

6. "Anglo-Welsh Poetry in the 1960s," *The Presence of the Past* (1987), 163.

7. The referendum of 1979 resulted in the defeat of a devolution proposal which would have granted Wales a measure of self-government.

CHRISTINE EVANS

Small Rain

The title refers to the second line of the famous middle English lyric, "Western Wind": "O western wind, when wilt thou blow? / The small rain down can rain."

the nunnery scene: in *Hamlet*, Act III.

Larkin's arrow-shower: in Philip Larkin's *The Whitsun Weddings*, an image of sexual potency and fertility.

Rhiannon: an important character in the First and Third Branches
of *The Mabinogi* and a fairly common name in contemporary Wales.
In the tale, the Birds of Rhiannon sing over the sea near Harlech,
waking the dead and sending the living to sleep.

rain in Wales: western areas, especially, are well known for having
very high rainfall.

Llŷn

The title refers to the narrow peninsula that juts out from
Gwynedd, enclosing Cardigan Bay to the south and pointing like an
arm across the Irish Sea—from where many of its early settlers
came. The name itself refers to "men of Leinster," and there is
archaeological evidence of the area's trading importance from
ancient times. Today it is remote and unspoiled.

Abergwaun . . . Cernyw . . . Llydaw: Welsh names are used for sev-
eral important links in the Celtic network: Abergwaun is Fishguard,
a harbour in Pembrokeshire; Cernyw is Cornwall; and Llydaw is
Britanny.

Second Language

selki people: seals that can take on human form, a common folktale
in the west of Britain. If trapped without their own skin, they always
long for the freedom of the sea and suffer a slow withering of spirit.
a boy riding a name out of myth: a reference to Teyrnon, "master of
horses" in the First Branch of *The Mabinogi*.

TONY CONRAN

Giants

"Giants," "Counting Song," "Caernarfon Across the Brown
Fields," and "Gwales" are part of a poem sequence titled "Castles."

Tre'r Ceiri: Literally, the town of the giants, Tre'r Ceiri is a splen-
didly preserved hill fort in the Llŷn peninsula in west Gwynedd,
high on one of the hills called yr Eifl, or the Rivals.

Counting Song

> Monasteries . . . : At Conwy the Pope's permission had to be obtained to move a monastery from the site to about six miles up river.

> Whole townlands . . . : At Beaumaris a Welsh town had to be evacuated to make room for the castle and its English walled town. Its inhabitants settled at Newborough (Niwbwrch) on the other side of Anglesey.

> The King's Peace: While Welsh law was founded on deciding between different claims to justice, English law was based on "keeping the king's peace."

> prophecies: During periods of national decline and oppression, Welsh poets tended to write messianic prophesies about the deliverer who would drive the enemy (usually the English) into the sea. Cadwaladr or Arthur or Owain would rise from the dead and return his people to their former greatness.

Caernarfon Across Brown Fields

> Which *Wledig*, Macsen or Cystennin . . . : Wledig (from Gwledig) is an early Welsh term meaning the ruler of a *gwlad*, a land or country. As a title it is largely reserved for a few figures in early Welsh tradition. Macsen Wledig is the Emperor of Rome in *The Dream of Macsen Wledig*, in *The Mabinogion*. Cystennin "succeeded his father as King of Britain and with Roman help conquered Macsen" (*The Oxford Companion to the Literature of Wales*, 1986).

Gwales

> Gwales (also Grassholm) is an island off the coast of Pembrokeshire in southwest Wales. In the Second Branch of *The Mabinogi*, seven Welshmen "returning from the campaign in Ireland spend eighty years on the island, with the head of Bendigeidfran (Brân), without aging or any recollection of their former sorrows" (*The Oxford Companion to the Literature of Wales*, 1986).

The three ravens will fly: Refers to the flag of Rhys ap Thomas when he marched through Wales to give crucial support to Henry Tudor at Bosworth.

Elegy for the Welsh Dead, in The Falkland Islands, 1982
"Y Gododdin": One of the earliest postclassical vernacular poems in Europe, perhaps dating to the sixth century A.D., "Y Gododdin" is a series of elegies for the three hundred picked men of a warband who, under Mynyddog Mwynfawr, chief of the British tribe called the Gododdin, launched a counterattack against Anglo-Saxon invaders. "Elegy for the Welsh Dead . . ." echoes elements of this ancient poem.

our boys: how Prime Minister Thatcher referred to the soldiers sent to fight the Falklands War.

fasces of tribunes: a bundle of rods with an axe in the middle carried before a high magistrate in Rome. A tribune was an officer who represented the Roman plebs, as opposed to the patrician consul. Therefore, by analogy, a member of the House of Commons.

Dragons: The flag of Cadwaladr, the legendary last king of all Britain before the Anglo-Saxon conquest, was the Red Dragon. This was the flag used by the Welshman Henry Tudor in his campaign to become Henry VII of England. It then became the Welsh flag.

RUTH BIDGOOD
Kindred
Molinia grass: tough, tussocky mountain grass.

low broken walls: In the upland solitudes there are remains of small houses, some of them "summer dairies" from the days of seasonal migration with flocks and herds.

Banquet
Scratting . . . wool: Hand-picking women are still to be found

lodging at remote farms and making a meager living by collecting wool caught on bushes or fences.

crowds who wept and begged and leapt: Reactions to charismatic evangelists were extreme, including jumping, crying aloud, even fits.

Llanfihangel
> The Victorian church of Abergwesyn. Its remains were carted away in 1963.

DUNCAN BUSH

Ramsey Island
> The title refers to an island off the Pembrokeshire coast, southwest Wales.

Summer 1984
> The title refers to the summer of the year-long miners' strike, 1984–85. The image of drowned valleys for the making of reservoirs is a potent one in Wales.

> The old men's proud and bitter / tales of 1926: refers to the miners' strike of that year.

JOHN BARNIE

Out of the Fight
> The black graves of the Cymry: Gravestones in Welsh Nonconformist chapels are often made of black slate. Cymry: the Welsh.

The Town Where I was Born
> The town is Abergavenny, Gwent, on the southeast border of Wales.

> Blorenge: a hill which is part of the scarp dividing Abergavenny and the Usk Valley from the industrial and coal mining valleys of south Wales to the west.

blast furnaces in the town beyond: a reference to the large iron and steel complex at Ebbw Vale about ten miles from Abergavenny over the scarp. The orange flickering glow of the furnaces could be seen at night reflected on the underside of clouds. The steelworks is now closed down.

Craig-y-Pistyll, Bryn Garw: hills in the Cambrian Mountains in the hinterland of Aberystwyth, Dyfed, in mid-Wales.

Banc-y-Darren, Cefn Llwyd: hamlets on approach slopes to the Cambrian Mountains, near Aberystwyth.

Pumlumon: the highest peak in mid-Wales.

Mynydd Epynt: a range of hills in mid-Wales.

I remembered how in Cardiff after the war . . . : a reference to the ruined streets in Cardiff, south Wales, after German bombing raids during World War II.

At Craig-y-Pistyll
literally, Waterfall Rock.

Salem: a hamlet about two miles from Craig-y-Pistyll.

INTERVIEW WITH JOHN BARNIE

1. Launched in 1970 by Ned Thomas and Sara Erskine, *Planet* ceased publication with its fiftieth issue in 1979. It resumed in 1985.

2. See Barnie's review article "The Anglo-Welsh Tradition" in *The King of Ashes* (1989).

3. A poet, short-story writer, novelist, critic, and scholar, Bobi Jones learned Welsh as a schoolboy.

4. Dramatist, poet, critic, political activist, and founder of Plaid Cymru (the Welsh Nationalist Party), Saunders Lewis is a preeminent Welsh literary figure of the twentieth century.

5. The Welsh Language Society, formed in 1962 to help prevent the extinction of the Welsh language.

MIKE JENKINS

Chartist Meeting

The Chartists were members of a nineteenth-century movement in Wales who campaigned, marched, and organized for a charter of rights, including male suffrage and trade union recognition. They were led for the most part by skilled workers like Morgan Williams (from Heolgerrig, above Merthyr Tudful) and often met in open-air, mountain-top locations.

Returning to the Nant

Nant Gwrtheyrn: an abandoned slate mining village on the coast of the Llŷn Peninsula, now renovated as the Welsh Language Center. "Gwrtheyrn" is the Welsh name for Vortigern, a fifth-century Brythonic king.

Ar Werth: For Sale.

Cymraeg: the Welsh language.

Saesneg: the English language.

butty: mate or buddy.

Gurnos Boy

"Gurnos Boy" and "Among the Debris" are written in Merthyr dialect, which is also, largely, the dialect of the south Wales valleys. Gurnos council estate: reputedly the second largest in Europe.

MAGIC MUSH: hallucinogenic fungi found seasonally on the mountains around Merthyr Tudful.

Among the Debris

The poem focuses on the lasting psychological effects of the Aberfan disaster of 21 October 1966, when a coal tip slid onto a primary school down valley from Merthyr Tudful (see also the note to Jean Earle's poem "Old Tips").

ROBERT MINHINNICK

The Drinking Art

Merthyr / And the Spanish foundrymen: Because of its iron foundries, Merthyr Tudful attracted workers from different areas of Europe during the early decades of this century.

The Looters

The poem is based on two major snowfalls of the 1980s, which closed the M4—the main south Wales roadlink—for some days.

Bedlinog: ex-mining village in south Wales.

Cwm Nash: feature of the "Glamorgan Heritage Coast" in south Wales. A "cwm" is a valley.

Development Area

The title is taken from the designation, or "status," given to much of Wales in the 1980s in an attempt to encourage economic regeneration and boost employment.
Crymlyn: a large fen on the edge of Swansea threatened by industrial expansion and waste tipping.

'What's the Point of Being Timid When the House Is Falling Down?'

The title is from a postcard the author received from poet John Tripp (1927–86), the subject of this poem.
Fescue: a type of grass.

Merthyr Road . . . Whitchurch: the area of Cardiff where John Tripp lived.

The Mansion

The poem is set at Cwrt Colman, Penyfai, the village where the poet was brought up, a place for children to trespass. For generations, the mansion and estate had provided employment for village people. The poem refers to the "refurbishment" of the mansion as a hotel.

the black nugget of poison: Yew berries are poisonous.

The Stones Themselves

The poem is set at the "Stones" museum, a very small exhibit room at Margam Park, south Wales.

This globe-woman: a Sheila na Gig (see the note to Gillian Clarke's "Sheila na Gig at Kilpeck.")

Looking for Arthur

The poem is set in an isolated area known as "Llanbad" (Church of Peter) on Mynydd y Gaer in mid-Glamorgan, where the walls of a church and part of a graveyard remain. The place has been described by maverick historians as the resting place of a chieftain who might have been King Arthur. Caves in the area are said to hold his knights/supporters.

Wellies: wellington boots.

SHEENAGH PUGH

The Frozen Field

Maldon: in Essex, England, site of a battle between the Anglo-Saxons and the Vikings in 991, the subject of the Old English poem "The Battle of Maldon."
Wulfmaer: kinsman of Byrhtnoth in "The Battle of Maldon."

Clontarf: outside Dublin, scene of a great tenth-century battle described in the Icelandic "Njal's Saga."

Arbela: one of Alexander the Great's Persian battles.

Sedgemoor: in Dorset, England, scene of a bloody battle in 1685 between the forces of James II and the Duke of Monmouth.

Solferino: in Italy, the battle which led to the founding of the Red Cross.

Aughrim: in Ireland, where William of Orange defeated James II.

Magenta: in Italy, a French/Italian victory over Austria.

Frankincense

> This poem is spoken by the vicar of a church near Sedgemoor, site of the battle described in the note to "The Frozen Field" (see above). The local men were on the losing (Monmouth) side. Their bodies were dumped in the church for a week or so to fester; the vicar later used the incense to get rid of the stench.

Railway Signals

> wide street / going nowhere: Bute Street, leading down to the now largely disused Cardiff docks.

TONY CURTIS

Pembrokeshire Seams

> Landsker: the geographical and demographical line which divides north Welsh-speaking Pembrokeshire from anglophone south Pembrokeshire.

> Range Rover: a four-wheel drive auto much loved by the middle and upper classes with homes and second homes in the country. Rebecca: the name taken by nineteenth-century rebels in their guerilla fight known as the "Rebecca Riots."

INTERVIEW WITH MEIC STEPHENS

> 1. Represented in this anthology under the name Tony Conran.

CATHERINE FISHER

St Tewdric's Well

> Bran: the king of the Isle of Britain in the Second Branch of *The Mabinogi*, of gigantic build.

Immrama

> Early Irish stories of fabulous sea voyages.

PETER FINCH

Rubbish

    CYMRU: Wales.

    Max Boyce: a Welsh singer/entertainer.

HILARY LLEWELLYN-WILLIAMS

Birch

    In the Celtic calendar/alphabet based on the names of trees, the first month after the winter solstice was the birch month. This poem is from a sequence based on that calendar.

To the Islands

    Llanybydder: a small market town in the valley of the river Teifi in west Wales. The "islands" created by the mist recall the legendary islands to the west in Welsh (and Irish, Scottish, Cornish, and Breton) mythology.

Brynberllan

    The title means "Orchard Hill." Local tradition maintains that the area had once been rich in orchards; none now remain.

    the stream called *Comely* and the stream / called *Blossom*: The names of the two streams have been translated: they are *Glwydeth* and *Blodau*.

    soul-fires: were lit at Calan Gaeaf or Samhain, on 1 November, All Soul's Day in the Christian calander, preceded by what is now called Halloween.

    a place of apple orchards: The reference is to Avalon (from *Afallon*, ultimately derived from Welsh *afall*, "apple"), the Land of Youth or the Isles of the Blessed.

Nola

    This is the first poem in a sequence based on the life and ideas of the sixteenth-century magus and philosopher Giordano Bruno.

Here Bruno is a young child conducting us on a tour of Nola, his native town, near Naples.

The Inner Artificer
This poem is the fourth in the sequence described in the note for "Nola," above.

R. S. THOMAS
R. I. P.
1988 marked the fourth centenary of the Bible's translation into Welsh by William Morgan (1545–1604), vicar of Llanrhaiadr ym Mochnant. This translation "is the foundation stone on which modern Welsh literature has been based" (*The Oxford Companion to the Literature of Wales*, 1986). Henry VIII's purpose in ordering the translation and the placing of a copy of it in every church in Wales was for the better promotion of an understanding of the English Bible. At the time of the 1988 centenary, a pilgrimage was made to Morgan's birthplace near Betws y Coed, Gwynedd. All the effort in translating and promoting, and all the enthusiasm of a pilgrimage, are contrasted with the Bible's present status, which is to gather dust on the window sill.
capital of the world: to an Englishman, the capital of the world is London.

the grinding of Hebrew / to Welsh corn: Morgan translated the Old Testament directly from the Hebrew.

▪ BIOGRAPHIES ▪

JOHN BARNIE
Born in Abergavenny, Wales, in 1941, John Barnie taught for thirteen years at Copenhagen University before returning to Wales in 1982. His most recent books include *Clay* (1989), a poem sequence; *The King of Ashes* (1989), a collection of essays; *The Confirmation* (1992), a collection of poetry and fiction; *Y Felan a Finnau: Golwg ar Hanes y Blues* (*The Blues and Me: A Look at the History of the Blues*), a study of blues music published in the Welsh language (1992); and *The City* (1993), a collection of poetry and fiction. Barnie lives in Comins Coch, near Aberystwyth in west Wales, where he edits *Planet, the Welsh Internationalist*, an English-language Welsh literary and cultural magazine.

CHRIS BENDON
Chris Bendon was born in Leeds, England, in 1950 and educated at St. David's University College in Lampeter, Wales. The author of eleven books and pamphlets, his most recent full-length book of poems, *Constructions*, was published in 1990. His poetry has appeared widely in magazines in the United States, Wales, and England. Bendon has received numerous prizes and awards, including First Prize in the Scottish Open Poetry Competition (Hugh MacDiarmid Memorial Trophy) and the WWF/*Guardian* Poetry Competition. He lives in Lampeter, Wales.

RUTH BIDGOOD
Ruth Bidgood was born in 1922 at Severn Sisters, Glamorganshire, Wales, and educated at Port Talbot and St. Hugh's College, Oxford. After living with her family in London for many years, she returned to Wales in 1964, when she began writing poetry and local history. Her collections of poetry include *The Given Time* (1972), *Not Without Homage* (1975), *The Print of Miracle* (1978), *Lighting Candles* (1982), *Kindred* (1986), and *Selected Poems* (1992), runner-up for the Welsh Arts Council Book of the Year, 1993.

DUNCAN BUSH

Duncan Bush was born in Cardiff, Wales, in 1946, and educated at Warwick University and Wadham College, Oxford. He currently directs the writing program at Gwent College, Wales, dividing his time between Wales and Luxembourg, where his wife teaches. Bush has published in a variety of genres, including poetry collections *Aquarium* (1983), *Salt* (1985), and *Black Faces, Red Mouths* (1986); a novel, *Glass Shot* (1991); two radio plays, *Are There Still Wolves in Pennsylvania?* (1990) and *In the Pine Forest* (1992), and a TV play, *Sailing to America* (1993).

GILLIAN CLARKE

Gillian Clarke was born in 1937 in Cardiff. She has published five collections of poems: *The Sundial* (1978), *Letter from a Far Country* (1982), *Selected Poems* (1985), *Letting in the Rumour* (1989), and *The King of Britain's Daughter* (1993). She has also translated from the Welsh a collection of traditional stories for children, *One Moonlit Night* (1991). An assistant editor of *The Anglo-Welsh Review* from 1971 to 1976, Clarke was editor from 1976 to 1984. In recent years, she has become well known in Wales for her work as a teacher of creative writing. She lives near Llandysul, in mid-Wales.

TONY CONRAN

Tony Conran was born in Bengal, India, in 1931 and lived in Liverpool, England, and Colwyn Bay, Wales, as a boy. He was educated at the University College of Wales, Bangor, and worked as a clerk in Chelmsford and as a university tutor in Bangor, taking early retirement in 1981. His critical study *The Cost of Strangeness: Essays on the English Poets of Wales* appeared in 1982. A noted translator, his *The Penguin Book of Welsh Verse* (1967) has recently been reissued by Seren Books as *Welsh Verse* (1992). Conran's recent poetry collections include *Spirit Level* (1974), *Life Fund* (1979), *Blodeuwedd* (1988), and *Castles* (1993).

TONY CURTIS

Tony Curtis was born in Carmarthen, Wales, in 1946 and educated at the University College, Swansea, and Goddard College, Vermont. He has published a number poetry collections, including *The Last Candles* (1989) and *Selected Poems* (1986). A new collection, *War Voices: War Poems 1970–1995*, is due out in 1995. The founder/editor of the magazine *Madog* and founder/publisher of Edge Press, Curtis has also edited a number of critical and literary anthologies, including *The Art of Seamus Heaney* (1982) and *Wales: The Imagined Nation* (1986). He is senior lecturer in English at the Polytechnic of Wales and lives in Barry, south Wales.

JOHN DAVIES

Born in 1944 in Cymmer, near Port Talbot, south Wales, John Davies was educated at University College, Aberystwyth. A schoolteacher living in Prestatyn, north Wales, he has taught in Michigan and Washington, and during 1987–88 was a visiting professor of poetry at Brigham Young University, Utah. He has published four collections of poetry: *At the Edge of Town* (1981), *The Silence in the Park* (1982), *The Visitor's Book* (1984), and *Flight Patterns* (1991). His third collection was joint winner of the Poetry Society's Alice Hunt Bartlett Award in 1986. Davies has edited a number of anthologies, including *The Green Bridge* (1988), short stories from Wales.

JEAN EARLE

Jean Earle was born in Bristol, England, in 1909, but brought up in the Rhondda Valley, south Wales, and educated at the College of Education, Cardiff. A housewife while her two daughters were growing up, she worked in various jobs afterwards: in legal and diocesan offices and as a writer and radio broadcaster. She published journalism and short stories when young and her first poetry at the age of seventy-one. Her poetry collections include *A Trial of Strength* (1980), *The Intent Look* (1984), *Visiting Light* (1988), and *Selected Poems* (1990). She lives in Shrewsbury.

CHRISTINE EVANS

Christine Evans was born in 1943 in Yorkshire to a family with a Welsh-speaking grandmother. She has taught English in Pwllheli since 1967. With her fisherman husband and son, she lives on a farm in the extreme west of the Llŷn Peninsula in north Wales. Evans has published two collections of poetry: *Looking Inland* (1983) and *Cometary Phases* (1989), and a long poem, *Falling Back* (1986). *Island of Dark Horses* is her forthcoming poetry collection.

PETER FINCH

A poet, performer, literary entrepreneur, editor, and critic, Peter Finch was born in 1947 in Cardiff, Wales, where he still lives. He is the founder/editor of the magazine *Second Aeon* (1966–74) and director, since 1973, of Oriel, the Welsh Arts Council Bookshop. The author of over twenty collections of poetry, including *Selected Poems* (1987), Finch's most recent collection is *Poems for Ghosts* (1991).

CATHERINE FISHER

Catherine Fisher was born in 1957 in Newport, Wales, where she currently lives. Her first collection of poetry is *Immrama* (1988); her second collection is due out in 1994. Fisher is also the author of *The Conjuror's Game, Fintan's Tower,* and *The Snow Walker's Son,* fantasy novels for children incorporating elements of Welsh myth.

JEREMY HOOKER

Jeremy Hooker was born near Southampton, England, in 1941. He moved in 1965 to Wales, to lecture at the University College of Wales at Aberystwyth, where he became an active reviewer and critic of Anglo-Welsh literature. In 1984 Hooker moved to live in the Netherlands; currently, he lives in Frome, England, and teaches at Bath College of Higher Education. The author of numerous critical studies of modern poetry, Hooker is also one of the most acclaimed of contemporary English poets. His most recent book, *Their Silence a Language* (1993), is a collaboration with sculptor Lee Grandjean involving poetry and prose, sculpture and drawing.

MIKE JENKINS

Mike Jenkins was born in Aberystwyth, Wales, in 1953 and educated at the University College of Wales, Aberystwyth. His four collections of poetry include *The Common Land* (1981), *The Empire of Smoke* (1983), *Invisible Times* (1986), and *A Dissident Voice* (1990). He also co-edited *The Valleys* (1984, with John Davies), an anthology of writing from and about the valleys of Glamorgan and Gwent. He was editor of *Poetry Wales* from 1986 to 1992. Jenkins teaches at a secondary school in Merthyr Tudful, south Wales.

NIGEL JENKINS

Nigel Jenkins was born on a farm in Gower, south Wales, in 1949. On leaving school, he worked for four years as a newspaper reporter in the English midlands, and then, after a period of travel, studied literature and film at the University of Essex. For a short time after this he worked as a roustabout on a traveling circus in the United States. He returned to live in Wales in 1976 and has earned his living since then as a full-time writer and freelance lecturer, living in Mumbles, near Swansea. His volumes of poetry include *Song and Dance* (1981), *Practical Dreams* (1983), and *Selected Poems 1974–1989* (1990).

HILARY LLEWELLYN-WILLIAMS

Hilary Llewellyn-Williams was born in Kent, England, in 1951, of Welsh/Spanish parenthood. From 1970–73 she studied English literature at Southampton University. She settled in Wales in 1982 with her partner and two children and now works as a freelance tutor of creative writing and as a counsellor. Her first collection of poetry, *The Tree Calendar* (1987), won a Welsh Arts Council Prize. Her second collection, *Book of Shadows*, was published in 1990.

ROBERT MINHINNICK

Born in 1952 in Neath, south Wales, and brought up in the village of Penyfai, Robert Minhinnick is the information officer with the environmental organization Friends of the Earth Cymru (Wales). He is the author of five collections of poetry: *A Thread in the Maze* (1978), *Native Ground* (1979), *Life Sentences* (1983), *The Dinosaur Park* (1985), and *The Looters* (1989). His volume of essays, *Watching the Fire Eater* (1992), won the Welsh Arts Council's Book of the Year Award for 1993.

SHEENAGH PUGH

Sheenagh Pugh was born in Birmingham, England, in 1950, of Welsh/Irish parentage, and educated at Bristol University. She worked as a civil servant, trade union branch secretary, part-time lecturer in creative writing, and freelance writer and translator (mainly of seventeenth-century German poetry). Pugh has lived in Wales since 1971. Her poetry collections include *Crowded by Shadows* (1977), *What a Place to Grow Flowers* (1982), *Earth Studies and*

Other Voyages (1982), *Beware Falling Tortoises* (1987), *Selected Poems* (1990), and *Sing for the Taxman* (1993).

OLIVER REYNOLDS

Oliver Reynolds was born in 1957 in Cardiff, Wales. He took a degree in drama at the University of Hull and is currently working as a freelance writer in London. His three books of poetry are *Skevington's Daughter* (1985), *The Player Queen's Wife* (1987), and *The Oslo Tram* (1991). In 1985, Reynolds won the Arvon International Poetry Prize. He lives in London.

MEIC STEPHENS

Meic Stephens was born in 1938 at Treforest, near Pontypridd, Wales. He founded the magazine *Poetry Wales* in 1965 and was its editor for eight years. As literature director of the Welsh Arts Council from 1967 to 1990, he was to a great extent responsible for fostering the growth of contemporary literature in Wales, in both Welsh and English. Among his publications are the *Writers of Wales* series (80 volumes, 1970–), *Linguistic Minorities in Western Europe* (1976), *The Oxford Companion to the Literature of Wales* (1986), *A Dictionary of Literary Quotations* (1989), *The Oxford Illustrated Literary Guide to Great Britain and Ireland* (1992), and several anthologies.

R. S. THOMAS

R. S. Thomas was born in 1913 in Cardiff, Wales, and educated at the University College of Wales, Bangor, and St. Michael's College, Llandâf, where he received theological training. He was ordained as a priest in the Church in Wales in 1936, retiring in 1978. Thomas has published twenty-four volumes of poetry since 1946, including his *Collected Poems* (1993). He lives on the Llŷn Peninsula in northwest Wales.

· INDEX OF FIRST LINES ·